Archetecture

4-

12/19

Archetecture

INTERNATIONAL ARCHITECTURE & INTERIORS
Series directed by Matteo Vercelloni

NEW AMERICAN HOUSES

COUNTRY, SEA & CITIES

MATTEO VERCELLONI
EDITED BY SILVIO SAN PIETRO
PHOTOGRAPHS BY PAUL WARCHOL

EDIZIONI
L'ARCHIVOLTO

IDEAZIONE E CURA DEL PROGETTO
Silvio San Pietro
Matteo Vercelloni

TESTI
Matteo Vercelloni

FOTOGRAFIE
Paul Warchol

REDAZIONE
Matteo Vercelloni

PROGETTO GRAFICO
Morozzi & Partners

REALIZZAZIONE GRAFICA E IMPAGINATO
Marcella Bonacina
Albina Bonacina
Silvio San Pietro

TRADUZIONI
Andrew Ellis

SI RINGRAZIANO
Gli architetti e gli studi di progettazione per la cortese collaborazione e per aver fornito i disegni dei loro archivi.
We are grateful to the architects and designers who have kindly contributed to this project and have provided drawings
from their files.

[ISBN 88-7685-097-X]

© Copyright 1997
EDIZIONI L'ARCHIVOLTO
Via Marsala, 3 - 20121 Milano
Tel. 02/2901.0424 - 2901.0444
Fax 02/2900.1942 - 659.5552

I edizione novembre 1997

INDICE GENERALE
CONTENTS

PREFACE

Like its predecessor, this second installment of the series "International Architecture & Interiors" focuses on new home designs in America, taking its cue from the overall architecture rather than from just the interiors. If the apartments featured in the first book evoked a composite panorama of different American urban lifestyles, this collection of nineteen single-family houses of varying size offer a further exploration of the theme we took up last year, in terms both of the comparisons the two books provide on architectural idiom and expression, and on different poetics and design procedures, and of the period of time under examination (the last decade). Furthermore, we called upon the same photographer, Paul Warchol, to do the second book. The exacting and objective photography that characterized our previous installment *Urban Interiors in New York and USA* is applied once again to document the home in its entirety, therefore taking account of the building's physical rapport with its setting, the design of the facades and the internal layout, the construction details, the use and juxtaposition of materials, and not least the intelligent exploitation of light, which is one of the chief compositional tools in the works outlined here, and crucial also to Warchol's visual essay. Each house is extensively illustrated with floor plans, elevations, drawings, and construction details, in order to help the reader interpret the rich photographic essay; other useful information, including a description of materials and furnishings in each project is provided in the relative data sheets at the end of the book, together with the biographies of the architects.

The reflections on modern American home design covered by the first volume apply the architecture contained here, though it is worth pointing out that the independent, single-family home is one of America's most important building types, and has provided fertile soil for the country's great architects, from Thomas Jefferson in the late 1700s to Frank Gehry in our own times. The American home, and the single-family unit in particular, developed in different ideological terrain than its European counterpart. The need to accommodate the architecture in such an indomitable environment frequent spawned full-fledged ecosystems of a wholly independent self-sufficient nature, whose purpose – besides the purely architectural expression – were to make life more livable in an otherwise hostile context. As a result, in the States the home became a means of experimenting with composition and form, a way of exploring the man-building-context relationship in an architectural and environmental key. But there was also a symbolic aspect, given that the family home, standing on its own in the countryside or on a private lot in the town, is symbolic of the nuclear family, upon which American society is founded.

In order to obtain a historical and critical overview of the nineteen projects present here, it is worth taking a look at the development of American "villa" architecture, to understand why we do not use this term to refer to these home designs from the last decade.

In his fundamental work on this type of architecture,[1] James Ackerman defines the villa as a building set in the countryside, designed principally as a retreat for the pleasure of its owner; the pleasure factor is what distinguishes it from the farmstead and its land, which is for agricultural use. Farmhouses, he points out, tend to be simpler in design and reiterate traditional building practices, often without calling on an architect. The villa, however, is a typical product of the architect's creativity, and cannot really be seen without some relation to city life, in the sense that it is not a separate entity, but a means for offsetting life in town, and therefore works as a satellite. The ideological significance of the villa, concludes Ackerman, therefore lies in the contrast between country and town, in which the virtues and pleasures of the former are like an antidote to the excesses of the latter.

Most of the project present here comply with Ackerman's assertions, and even the urban dwellings (Eric Cobb in Seattle, Michael Graves in Princeton, Smith Mille and Hawkinson in Los Angeles) rely on various intelligent expedients and devices to instill a sense of isolation from their urban surroundings. Nonetheless, we prefer to talk of these projects as "houses," and occasionally as "homes," rather that as "villas," a word that actually went out of use in America at the turn of the century, and was never in fact used by two of America's major architects, Henry Hobson Richardson,[2] and Frank Lloyd Wright[3] to describe their large extra-urban houses. Before outlining the background of the American villa and finding the reasons why this word was discarded by the architectural community, it is worth pointing out certain aspects of the building type that seem to have withstood time as architectural invariables of the genre.

6

[1] James S. Ackerman, The Villa. Form and Ideology of Country Houses, Princeton University Press, Princeton, New Jersey, 1990.

[2] See Witold Rybczynski's discussion of the implications of the word "home" in his study, Home. A Short HIstory of an Idea (Viking Pinguin, New Yokr 1986).

[3] The historian Kenneth Frampton used the term "house" for the title of his book on important house designs in American from the start ofthe century (Masterworks – The Twentieth-Century Houses, Rizzoli New York, 1995).

Ackerman stresses that the villa type is among the architectural types that are less obliged to comply with precise formulas, and hence can express and experiment new combinations and formal arrangements that do not stem from customs and styles of the past. More generally, the American home of whatever period strives to typify the cutting edge of modern design, even when, in the 1700s an attempt at revival was made (with the neo-Palladians of the circle of Lord Burlington), the outlook was distinctly progressive and even at times controversial with regard to the conventions followed by the status quo.

Ackerman identifies two basic classes of villa design: the cubic and compact type, and the open, articulated type. These two models of comparison have lasted since Roman times, and cover the many different manifestations of house design all over the world, and are therefore applicable as classes to the projects illustrated in this book.

The villa "type" in America was a legacy of the British colonists, who built large villas in the southern states especially at the heart of the cotton plantations. These were large manors that aimed to provide a comfortable and even luxurious lifestyle despite the hostile environment, which had to be governed. Stylistically, such houses tended to emphasize a lingering nostalgia for the homeland and for the style of life led by the English gentleman. In the northern states, however, except for the anomaly of the villas at Newport, the lack of a similar development of villa architecture – almost a caricature of the English mansion, transplanted to American soil – is due to the diversity of political and social background of the colonist population of the north, a situation that produced an altogether different "type" that looms large in American architectural history, namely, the cottage. The most radical change in the history of American architecture took place in the early 1800s, when the ideology of this building type was rendered more democratic, and made accessible to members of the rising middle classes. Leading exponents of this process of popularization were Alexander Jackson Davis (1803–92) and above all Andrew Jackson Downing (1815–52) who, translating into American the examples of the English landscape gardener Humphrey Repton and Richard Payne Knight, shifted the accepted type from that of the country manor (such as Jefferson's house at Monticello, 1769) toward a creative reworking of the farmstead. This crucial grammatical and symbolic shift, endorsed by a series of highly successful and widely read publications, spawned the new idea of the cottage as an "aestheticized" form of the traditional farmhouse and annexes. By means of the ideological transmogrification of the villa to the cottage, the middle classes were now in a position to express themselves without feeling any complex with regard to the wealthy landlords and landowners. Once the villa had been presented as a primary necessity, it was not long before people in the merchant classes began to build them, until they came to fill the suburbs of the larger cities, and subsequently of smaller towns. Eventually, the term "villa" itself came to be applied to any detached dwelling, or to the classic semidetached home with a dividing wall separating the two family units, whether such houses stood in the town, suburbs, or countryside, surrounded by an open space no larger than the front yard of houses in more densely built-up areas of town. This process of development, however, did not have a negative influence on the evolution of the villa in the traditional sense, except to cause the term to be devalued and used for any common-or-garden private dwelling. The work of Downing had a sweeping influence on the American way of conceiving and constructing homes; more than anyone else, he managed to draw the public away from the classicist grammar of the large country house, and steer tastes toward more organic and nature-oriented form of architecture, and with this, toward a national style. Without worry too much whether this was architecture of quality, and even stooping to easy eclecticism, Downing shepherded American house architecture on a course that would culminate with Richardson and Wright. Furthermore, another basic concept of American home design, was that a house should express the personality of its owner, as well as serve as a moral signpost for society. He argued that whoever managed to build a house that was finer than his neighbor's was contributing to the moral uplift of the society in which he lived. The adaptation of building design to the character and taste of the client is one of the critical factors for understanding the production of single-family homes in the United States since the beginning of this century, and today many of the examples presented in this book are the fruit of a careful adaptation to the personality of the future occupant. Frank Lloyd Wright, the undisputed father of modern American architecture, claimed that there ought to be as many different types of house as there are owners and personalities; the more a house has character, he averred, the more it improves with age. In this way he underscored that a house's design must mirror whoever lives in it.

The houses presented in this book belong firmly to this specifically American tradition, and testify directly to the continuity of a course of design that still offers plenty of opportunities for further development. Whether they are in the countryside or at the seashore, for vacations or just for the weekend break, or in the city as a residence of a special nature, the houses presented here undoubtedly reflect the personality of their occupant. Some of them constitute a rereading or reinvention of some of the traditional American ways of dealing with the problems of today's living. References to Thoreau's *Walden* (1845), a gospel for anyone who believes in the outdoor life and has a love of nature, can be found in some of the projects, in which the tradition of the cottage is imaginatively remodeled to create a new kind of retreat, ensconced in the depths of nature far from the madding crowd[4] (David Coleman at Lake Seymore, Marlys Hann in the Catskills, Peter Forbes in the woods of Mount Desert Island). The art of playing off tradition with imaginative new ideas is evident in the new summer home of Peter Samton on Fire Island, in the beach house designed by Steven Holl at Martha's Vineyard, an ingenious reworking of the balloon-frame building technique; also vying with tradition, in this case redefining the classic motifs of Italian villa architecture, is Michael Graves' new house in Princeton, in our opinion a design that is a far cry from the blaring postmodern style of which the architect was the unchallenged leader. Another issue that arises in the new homes chosen for this book is the problem of building on an existing building, and in this sense the houses designed by Peter Gluck in the countryside of Millerton and Worcester are sapient enlargements and extensions of farmhouses and relics of agricultural architecture. The house created by William Leddy inside an old barn in Chester County, involves the magical grafting of new and old, like a set of Russian dolls that fit one inside the other, resulting in a highly effective and lucid composition. Stamberg and Aferiat tackled the enlargement of an old country house in Sycamore Creek without forgoing their characteristic compositional flair, bringing the old and new closely together to create a series of engaging "inhabitable counterpoints."

The question of "restoring" modern buildings, now a hot issue in Europe too, is ably expressed here in the extension scheme designed by Smith Miller & Hawkinson for a house on the Los Angeles hillside. The original house was built in 1960 by Donald Plosky, who was a pupil of one of the masters of modern American architecture, Richard Neutra, known abroad particularly for a series of houses he built in the Los Angeles area. The other projects – entirely new houses sited in country, coast, or city have been construed as "microcities" through a modern rethinking of that legendary place the Villa Adriana at Tivoli (Diana Agrest and Mario Gandelsonas at Sagaponack). Their aim was to create a singular "inhabitable object," a concise medley of volumes and shapes emerging from nature (Edward Mills at Brighton, Schwartz & Silver at Copake, Studio Architrope at Canaan, Peter Gluck at Olive Bridge), and as new urban totems (Pasanella, Klein, Stolzman & Berg at Daytona Beach, Eric Cobb at Seattle), whose linguistic and figurative interplay illustrates the expressive freedom of the ongoing experiment in American contemporary house design – an architectural "type" that is hard to pin down, except to acknowledge its astonishing variety of composition, materials, and sheer design flair.

Matteo Vercelloni

4 *On the theme of retreats and small buildings set in woodland, see Gustau Gili Galletti, Casa Refugio Private Retreats, Editoriale Gustavo Gili, Barcelona, 1995).*

PREFAZIONE

Secondo volume della collana "International Architecture & Interiors", questo libro affronta, come il primo, il tema dei nuovi spazi domestici americani, spingendosi però nell'analisi di architetture complete e non solo a livello di progetti d'interni. Se gli appartamenti, oggetto del primo volume, hanno definito un composito panorama dei modi di abitare americani in città, crediamo che i diciannove progetti di case unifamiliari, di grandi e medie dimensioni, selezionati per questo libro offrano un diretto approfondimento del discorso iniziato un anno fa, sia per il sinergico confronto di linguaggi e figure, differenti poetiche e percorsi progettuali proposti, sia per l'arco di tempo esaminato (l'ultimo decennio), sia soprattutto per il medesimo autore dei servizi fotografici: Paul Warchol. La lettura fotografica rigorosa e oggettiva che ha caratterizzato gli interni presentati in *Urban Interiors in New York & U.S.A.* si ritrova anche in questo volume, dove l'obiettivo della macchina fotografica è chiamato questa volta a documentare spazi domestici in modo complessivo, cogliendo il senso del progetto di architettura nella sua globalità; dal volume della casa al rapporto con il paesaggio, dal disegno delle facciate alla distribuzione degli spazi, sino a scendere nella lettura di particolari costruttivi, a mettere in evidenza l'uso e il confronto dei materiali, a cogliere al meglio l'impiego della luce, strumento compositivo di grande importanza in tutti i progetti selezionati e affrontato ovviamente con particolare attenzione da Warchol. Tutte le case sono corredate da ricchi apparati iconografici composti da piante, sezioni, disegni di particolari costruttivi, che aiutano il lettore a capire i progetti illustrati nelle fotografie a colori, mentre utili informazioni, la descrizione di materiali e arredi impiegati nei singoli progetti sono riportate nella forma di schede descrittive a conclusione del volume, insieme con le biografie dei progettisti.

Le riflessioni sulla 'casa americana' contenute nella prefazione del primo volume sono valide anche per la comprensione di questi progetti, ma occorre ancora sottolineare come il tema della casa unifamiliare sia stato ed è in America una delle tipologie più importanti, uno dei capitoli basilari nella storia dell'architettura americana, terreno dove ogni grande architetto di questo paese si è cimentato con impegno e passione dal Settecento ad oggi, da Thomas Jefferson a Frank Gehry. La residenza americana, la casa unifamiliare in particolare, è cresciuta su un tessuto simbolico di valori diversi da quelli dell'omologo europeo; la necessità di doversi confrontare con una natura che difficilmente accetta di essere dominata ha prodotto costruzioni che si configurano come veri e propri ecosistemi, autonomi e compiuti, il cui scopo, al di là delle forme architettoniche prodotte, è quello di rendere vivibile un contesto altrimenti ostile o quasi per la vita dell'uomo. La casa è divenuta così in America il punto di riferimento di un processo di sperimentazione compositiva che studia il rapporto uomo-edificio-contesto risolvendolo in chiave architettonica e ambientale, ma anche simbolica, poiché la casa unifamiliare, la costruzione isolata nel paesaggio o in un piccolo lotto, è il simbolo principe del valore della famiglia, considerato da sempre nucleo della società americana.

Per comprendere dal punto di vista storico-critico i diciannove progetti che compongono questo libro occorre inoltre affrontare, sia pur brevemente, le vicende del tipo architettonico della 'villa' americana e del perché questo termine non viene da noi usato per descrivere queste qualificate architetture domestiche dell'ultimo decennio. Nel suo fondamentale e insuperato studio James S. Ackerman[1], definisce in questo modo il 'tipo' della villa: "Una villa è un edificio progettato per sorgere in campagna e finalizzato a soddisfare l'esigenza di svago e di riposo del suo proprietario. Benché essa possa costituire anche il nucleo di un'azienda agricola, l'elemento piacere è ciò che distingue la villa intesa come edificio residenziale dalla fattoria e i terreni ad essa collegati dalle terre a sfruttamento agricolo. La casa colonica tende a essere semplice nella struttura e a conservare forme inveteratamente tradizionali che non implicano l'intervento di un progettista. La villa è invece il prodotto tipico della capacità creativa di un architetto e ne documenta la modernità. [...] La villa non può essere compresa prescindendo dal suo rapporto con la città. Essa esiste infatti non per assolvere funzioni autonome, ma per controbilanciare valori e vantaggi della vita urbana, e la sua condizione economica è quella di un'entità satellite [...] Il significato ideologico della villa è radicato nel contrasto tra campagna e città, nel quale le virtù e i piaceri dell'una sono presentati in antitesi ai vizi e agli eccessi dell'altra." La maggior parte dei progetti presentati in questo libro rientrano in tali accezioni, e anche le costruzioni urbane (Eric Cobb a Seattle, Michael Graves a Princeton, Smith Miller e Hawkinson a Los Angeles) si pongono in vari modi come entità compiute e distinte rispetto al tessuto urbano da cui si distaccano con leggerezza, maestria e invenzione progettuale. Tuttavia preferiamo parlare di questi progetti come *houses*, o a

1. James S. Ackerman, The Villa. Form and Ideology of Country Houses, Princeton University Press, Princeton, New Jersey, 1990. Trad. It. La Villa - Forma e ideologia, Giulio Einaudi Editore, Torino 1992. Sul significato ideologico della villa, dal XVI secolo all'epoca del modernismo vedi anche R. Bentmann e M.Müller Die Villa als Herrschaftsarchitektur, syndikat autoren und verlagsgesellschaft, Francoforte 1970. Trad. it. Un proprio paradiso La villa: architettura del dominio, edizioni lavoro, Roma 1986.

volte meglio sarebbe dire *homes* [2], e non descriverli come "ville", termine che proprio in America cadde addirittura in disuso negli ultimi anni del secolo scorso e che non fu mai impiegato ad esempio da due dei maggiori architetti americani di residenze di campagna come Henry Hobson Richardson e Frank Lloyd Wright[3] per descrivere le loro grandi case extraurbane. Prima di accennare alle vicende della villa americana e di cercare le ragioni dell'abbandono di questo termine da parte della cultura architettonica di questo paese, ci preme sottolineare alcuni aspetti di questa forma abitativa che sembrano permanere con forza dall'antichità a oggi, quali invarianti architettoniche di riferimento. Ackerman sottolinea come il 'tipo' della villa, sia tra i 'tipi architettonici' quello meno vincolato a seguire regole formali precise e quindi a esprimere e a sperimentare nuove libertà compositive che non seguono mai consuetudini e stili del passato. Più comunemente la villa si sforza "di essere paradigma dello stile architettonico più attuale", nel rifiuto di un linguaggio predominante e anche quando ad esempio nel Settecento si è fatto ricorso alla pratica del *revival* (i neopalladiani inglesi del circolo di Lord Burlington) questo è avvenuto in senso progressista e polemico rispetto alle espressioni architettoniche del potere ufficiale. Sempre Ackerman individua due modelli di riferimento per l'architettura della villa: quello di forma cubica e compatta e quello di struttura aperta e articolata. Figure che permangono dall'antica Roma al presente, per dividere e confrontare in due grandi famiglie le molteplici espressioni di ville di ogni paese e che possiamo ancora ritrovare negli esempi contemporanei raccolti in questo libro.

La comparsa del 'tipo' della villa in America è dovuto ai coloni inglesi che edificarono grandi ville soprattutto negli stati meridionali all'interno delle piantagioni di cotone; ampie dimore che, nel riuscito tentativo di offrire una comoda e lussuosa abitazione pur all'interno di una natura ostile, da domare, sottolineavano allo stesso tempo dal punto di vista stilistico il legame culturale con l'Inghilterra e più in generale la nostalgia per i gusti della vita del gentiluomo inglese. Negli stati del nord invece, a eccezione del fenomeno esclusivo delle ville di Newport, l'assenza di uno sviluppo analogo della tipologia della grande villa, meccanica e caricaturale trasposizione di quella inglese in territorio americano, si deve alle differenti origine politiche e sociali dei colonizzatori che produssero un altro 'tipo' fondamentale per la storia dell'architettura americana: la casa colonica da cui si sviluppò poco dopo, e con grande diffusione, il *cottage*. Il mutamento più radicale nella storia della villa americana si verificò all'inizio dell'Ottocento, quando l'ideologia di questo tipo architettonico si democratizzò divenendo accessibile ai membri dei ceti urbani mediobassi in fase di crescita economica. Protagonisti di questo processo di divulgazione furono Alexander Jackson Davis (1803-92) e soprattutto Andrew Jackson Downing (1815-52) che, traducendo in chiave americana la lezione paesaggista inglese di Humphrey Repton e di Richard Payne Knight, spostarono il 'tipo' della villa dall'accezione della dimora di campagna in stile classico (la casa di Thomas Jefferson a Monticello del 1769) alla creativa rivisitazione della casa colonica del contadino. Da questo profondo slittamento grammaticale e simbolico, sostenuto da una serie di pubblicazioni diffuse capillarmente e con grande successo tra il grande pubblico, scaturì dal punto di vista architettonico il *cottage* quale forma estetizzata delle tradizionali fattorie e dei suoi edifici complementari. La "villa" (o meglio la sua trasformazione ideologica e stilistica nel *cottage*) diventa così con Downing lo strumento architettonico con cui la classe media poteva emulare e sfidare senza complessi la posizione privilegiata dei proprietari terrieri e dei ricchi possidenti. "Una volta che la villa era stata presentata come un prodotto di prima necessità, breve era stato il passo verso la sua costruzione da parte dei fautori del libero mercato e anche verso la sua produzione massificata alla periferia delle grandi città e, in ultimo anche delle piccole. [...] In definitiva il termine "villa" finì con l'essere applicato a ogni residenza isolata o a case generalmente bifamiliari con il solo muro divisorio in comune, in città, in periferia o in campagna, circondate da uno spazio aperto un poco più grande di quello solito alle abitazioni prospicienti le strade densamente popolate dei quartieri centrali delle città. Questo processo di sviluppo, tuttavia, non influenzò negativamente l'evoluzione della villa intesa in senso tradizionale se non forse svilendo il significato della parola "villa", ora usata per designare anche un tipo di abitazione modesto e dozzinale"[4]. L'opera di Downing ebbe un'influenza enorme sul modo americano di concepire e costruire le abitazioni, più di chiunque altro egli allontanò il grande pubblico dal classicismo, inteso come unica grammatica per costruire le grandi case di campagna, per indirizzarlo verso un'architettura organicamente legata alla natura; in sostanza verso la ricerca di un linguaggio nazionale. Anche se non si preoccupò troppo che questa fosse un'architettura di qualità, sposando anche la prati-

2. Come afferma Witold Rybczynski nel suo studio Home A short History of an Idea, Viking Pinguin, New York 1986. Trad. It. La Casa, Rusconi Libri, Milano 1989: "Questa parola meravigliosa, home, che designa un luogo materiale, ma anche una più astratta sensazione personale, non ha equivalenti nelle lingue latine o slave. I tedeschi, i danesi, gli svedesi, gli islandesi, gli olandesi e gli inglesi hanno parole dallo stesso suono per home, tutte derivate dall'antico norvegese heima. [...] La parola home ha sommato in sé il significato di casa e quello di famiglia, di abitazione e di rifugio, di proprietà e di valore affettivo. Home sta a significare tanto la casa, con tutto quello che a essa è connesso, quanto le persone che vi abitano e la conseguente sensazione di intimità. L'abitazione può cambiare, ma si finisce sempre per tornare "a casa" (home)."

3. Anche lo storico contemporaneo Kenneth Frampton per intitolare il suo studio comparativo delle maggiori residenze americane dall'inizio del secolo ad oggi (American Masterworks-The Twentieth Century Houses, Rizzoli New York, 1995) impiega nel titolo il termine House a testimoniare come la parola "Villa" sia intesa in senso decadente e vetusto nella terminologia critico-storica americana.

4. James S. Ackerman, Op.cit.

ca dell'eclettismo a buon mercato, Downing mise la nazione su un percorso che doveva culminare nelle conquiste di Richardson e Wright. Inoltre, altro concetto basilare della cultura dell'abitazione americana, per Downing la casa era espressione dell'individualità e della personalità del proprietario, oltre che configurarsi come strumento di moralizzazione della società: "Colui che presenta al pubblico un modello di abitazione più bello e raffinato rispetto a quello dei suoi vicini di casa, è un benefattore della causa della moralità e del buon ordine ed è artefice del miglioramento della società in cui vive"[5]. L'adattamento del progetto architettonico al carattere e al gusto del singolo cliente è un concetto fondamentale per comprendere la produzione delle case unifamiliari americane dall'inizio del secolo a oggi e molti degli esempi raccolti in questo volume sono progetti redatti in stretta sintonia con il carattere e la personalità del committente. Frank Lloyd Wright, padre indiscusso dell'architettura moderna americana, affermava che devono esserci tanti tipi di case, quanti sono i tipi di uomini e di personalità e che più una casa ha carattere proprio, più acquista valore invecchiando; sottolineando così come la casa dovesse essere necessariamente specchio dell'individualità di chi vi abita.

Le case presentate in questo libro rientrano pienamente in questa specifica tradizione americana, costituendo una testimonianza diretta e sottolineando la continuità di un percorso progettuale tuttora di grande interesse. Costruite in campagna e al mare, per le vacanze e per i week-end, in città come residenze d'eccezione, queste case rispecchiano senza dubbio la personalità dei loro abitanti, a volte rileggendo e reinventando molte tradizioni della cultura americana nell'affrontare temi e problematiche contemporanei. Ad esempio, la memoria del testo di Henry D. Thoreau, *Walden; or Life in the Woods,* (1845), riferimento per ogni cultore della vita all'aria aperta e per gli amanti della natura, ricorre in alcuni dei progetti esaminati in cui la figura e la tradizione del *cottage* viene rielaborata con creatività per definire nuove case-rifugio[6], lontane dal frastuono urbano e calate con attenzione nel verde (David Coleman a Lake Seymore, Marlys Hann sui monti di Catskills, Peter Forbes nei boschi di Mount Desert Island). L'aspetto del confronto con la tradizione e della sua creativa reinvenzione emerge nella residenza estiva di Peter Samton a Fire Island, nella casa sulla spiaggia progettata da Steven Holl a Martha's Vineyard, una rigorosa rivisitazione della pratica costruttiva del *balloon frame*; nella ridefinizione di figure proprie della villa all'italiana a opera di Michael Graves a Princeton, un progetto ben lontano a nostro avviso dagli spenti clamori postmoderni di cui l'architetto del New Jersey fu indiscusso protagonista. Ancora emerge in alcuni dei progetti selezionati la problematica contemporanea del 'costruire sul costruito': le case progettate da Peter Gluck nelle campagne di Millerton e di Worcester si configurano come sapienti e raffinati ampliamenti di fattorie e costruzioni legate al lavoro agricolo. Quella pensata da William Leddy all'interno di un antico granaio a Chester County appare come magico *innesto nella storia,* sorta di abile 'matrioska architettonica', di grande efficacia e lucidità compositiva. Stamberg e Aferiat hanno affrontato un ampliamento di una vecchia casa di campagna a Sycamore Creek senza rinunciare alla raffinata sperimentazione compositiva che è loro propria avvicinando il vecchio e il nuovo in una riuscita sintesi di 'contrappunti abitabili'.

Il tema del 'restauro del moderno', di grande attualità anche in Europa, viene ben espresso nel progetto di ampliamento a opera di Smith Miller e Hawkinson di una casa sulle colline di Los Angeles, costruita nel 1960 da Donald Plosky, allievo di Richard Neutra, maestro dell'architettura moderna americana, riconosciuto a livello internazionale proprio per la progettazione di una fortunata serie di residenze unifamiliari angelene. Gli altri progetti, case costruite ex-novo in campagna, al mare e in città, pensati come 'microcittà', rivisitazione in chiave contemporanea del tema-mito della Villa Adriana di Tivoli (Diana Agrest e Mario Gandelsonas a Sagaponack), come eccezionali oggetti abitabili, sintesi volumetriche e scultoree emergenti dalla natura (Edward Mills a Brighton, Schwartz e Silver a Copake, Studio Architrope a Canaan, Peter Gluck a Olive Bridge) e come nuovi segni urbani (Pasanella, Klein, Stolzman e Berg a Daytona Beach, Eric Cobb a Seattle), sottolineano nel loro confronto linguistico e figurativo la ricchezza e la libertà espressiva della continua sperimentazione architettonica compiuta nell'ambito della progettazione della casa americana contemporanea; un 'tipo architettonico' difficilmente codificabile, se non per straordinaria ricchezza compositiva e cura del dettaglio, scelte materiche e passione progettuale.

Matteo Vercelloni

5. Andrew Jackson Downing, The Architecture of Country Houses, 1850. Edizione anastatica, New York 1968.

6. Sul tema della casa come rifugio e piccola architettura isolata nel verde, nell'ambito della cultura architettonica moderna e contemporanea vedi: Gustau Gili Galletti, Casas Refugio Private Retreats, Editoriale Gustavo Gili, Barcellona 1995.

MICROCITTA'
MICROCITY

D. Agrest & M. Gandelsonas Architects with Claire Weisz
Interiors by Wal Siskind. Sagaponack, Southampton, New York

The concept of the "villa" as a grouping of living elements, spaces, and volumes – discerningly interlocking to form strict symmetries or dynamic downscaled urban landscapes – has its roots in the distant past. One of the various possible models taken by contemporary architects worldwide, Americans included, is Hadrian's Villa at Tivoli near Rome.[1] This project for a holiday home in Southampton, New York, designed for an art collector, seems to take its cue from

the villa model, starting with the name itself, Villa Amore, and in the actual design process, which has engendered a composite and multi-faceted building, indeed almost an architectural *summa* that is informed with a calibrated and only apparently contradictory merger with local references (the famous shingle technique of horizontal wooden sidings), combined with forms that remold standard forms of modern architecture with elementary geo-metrical volumes. The outcome is a large unit with a wooden barrel-vaulted ceiling, a space on which pivot various elements and rooms, each one different and with a self-sufficient character. Vaguely transparent cylindrical towers with echoes of the Bauhaus or scaled-down lighthouses, singular-looking blocks and suspended units that proliferate in a skillful compilation of *objets trouvés* framing the backdrop of farmlands, rather than forming a cohesive whole. In this respect, the long timber catwalk that terminates in a suspended wooden gazebo offers an almost abstract shape cut against the blue sky, posing as a magical belvede-re – a requisite of any villa, of whatever age or clime. Diversity is also expressed in the doors and windows. There are horizontal band apertures *à la* Corbusier, square or vertical windows that allow different perceptions of the surrounding landscape from each room of the house. The interiors, designed by Wal Siskind, underscore the timber theme announced by the facade. The layout consists of two distinct sections: on the ground story, beneath the vaulted roof, are grouped the daytime environments, with living room, dining room, kitchen, and breakfast area, reading room, and a small greenhouse. Accessed via spiral stairways are the towers that start from the first story, their catwalk-bridges skewed from the main building below, emphasizing the two primary geometries of the complex, while expressing the distorted perspective declared by the wedge-shaped entrance. The towers are interlinked via lower units, and house the various night zones, the private quarters of the owners, and the guest suites, all giving onto terraces of a kind, and suspended walkways with a gazebo. The structure is lar-gely in timber, with additions of metal and masonry. These inserts are particularly noticeable in the stand-alone pool section, where a striking white wall sunders two small wood constructions enclosing changing rooms and service facilities. The result is a micro-city, if you like, a kind of understated eclecticism in a modern key that emerges as a persuasive architectural aggregation from the tended fields of the countryside, a house that is at once "classical and romantic, formal and poetic. The designers themselves have stated that Villa Amore shuns stylistic classification and hovers between the abstract and figurative, between convention and idiosyncrasy".

1. Charles Moore, one of the leading American postmoden-ists, defined Hadrian's Villa as a paradigm of noble eclecticism, whose composi-tional rules establish a formal dominion upon the landscape, confirming the subjective sense of the "architectural place".

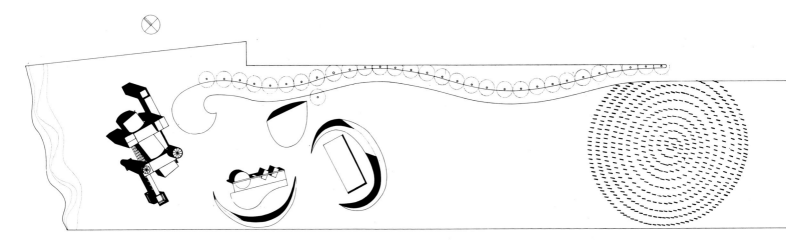

Site plan/ planivolumetrico

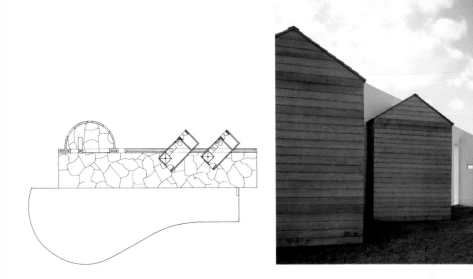

Il progetto della villa come insieme di elementi, spazi e volumi abitabili, connessi tra loro con grande maestria a formare rigide simmetrie o movimentati micropaesaggi urbani ha origini antiche. Tra i molti riferimenti quello di Villa Adriana a Tivoli è stato preso a modello da molti architetti anche americani, protagonisti dell'architettura contemporanea.[1] Anche questo progetto di una casa di vacanza nelle campagne di Southampton per un collezionista d'arte, sembra rifarsi a tale modello sia per il nome, "Villa Amore", sia per il procedimento progettuale, che ha portato alla definizione di un'architettura composita e dalle molte facce, una sorta di riuscita 'summa' architettonica che ha saputo fondere in una studiata e solo apparentemente contraddittoria sintesi abitabile riferimenti storici locali (le famose case Shingle Style costruite in legno e con facciate rivestite da assi orizzontali leggermente inclinate verso l'esterno per respingere l'acqua piovana) con figure che reinterpretano forme conosciute della storia dell'architettura moderna insieme a volumi geometrici elementari. Ecco allora che intorno a una costruzione centrale di riferimento, un grande spazio unitario coperto da una volta a botte di legno, si sviluppano e si aggregano altri elementi e altre stanze, diversi tra loro e compiuti nella loro figura individuale. Torri cilindriche più o meno trasparenti che ricordano il Bauhaus e fari in scala ridotta, volumi forti e piccole casette sospese si moltiplicano in una riuscita addizione di objets trouvés che incorniciano il paesaggio agricolo, più che presentarsi come in insieme omogeneo. In questo senso anche la lunga passerella di legno che si conclude con un moderno gazebo ligneo pensile, quasi una figura astratta che si staglia nell'azzurro del cielo, si propone come magico 'belvedere', complemento necessario alla villa di ogni età. Ancora, ogni apertura è diversa dalle altre; si trovano finestre a nastro orizzontali ispirate a Le Corbusier e finestre quadrate o verticali in modo da permettere una diversa esperienza di percezione del paesaggio esterno da ogni camera della casa. Gli interni, progettati da Wal Siskind, enfatizzano il carattere ligneo dominante sulle facciate. La distribuzione è divisa in due parti distinte; al piano terreno, sotto la grande volta, è organizzata la zona giorno con il soggiorno, la sala da pranzo, la cucina e la zona per il breakfast, sale di lettura e una piccola serra. Raggiungibili con diverse scale a chiocciola, le torri che si sviluppano al primo piano e i loro ponti sono ruotati rispetto alla costruzione sottostante sottolineando le due diverse geometrie primarie dell'impianto ed esprimendo allo stesso tempo la distorsione prospettica già percepita dall'ingresso a cuneo. Le torri, tra loro collegate da volumi più bassi, ospitano le diverse zone notte, gli appartamenti privati dei proprietari e le stanze degli ospiti, tutte affacciate su terrazze e terrazzini, percorsi pensili con gazebo. La costruzione è per la maggior parte di legno con aggiunta di parti metalliche e in muratura. Queste sono particolarmente evidenti nella zona a sé della piscina, dove un forte muro bianco taglia le due piccole costruzioni di legno che ospitano gli spogliatoi e i servizi. Sorta di governata e moderna espressione di nuovo eclettismo architettonico, questa microcittà che emerge come un convincente agglomerato architettonico dai prati coltivati della campagna ci appare "classica e romantica, formale e pittoresca". Come affermano gli stessi progettisti "Villa Amore si sforza di resistere alle classificazioni stilistiche e tipologiche, navigando tra dimensione astratta e figurativa, tra convenzione e idiosincrasia".

1. Charles Moore, uno dei protagonisti del movimento post moderno americano, definiva Villa Adriana come "paradigma di nobile eclettismo, da essa appare ricavata l'autorevole anomalia quale regola compositiva atta a stabilire un dominio formale sulla natura. Da essa ancora, risulta confermata l'intuizione soggettiva nella sedimentazione del 'luogo' architettonico". (In Perspecta n° 6, 1960).

North elevation / Prospetto nord

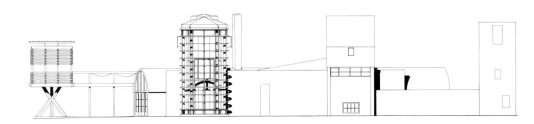

East elevation / Prospetto est

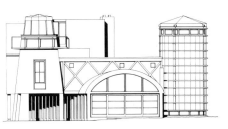

South elevation / Prospetto sud

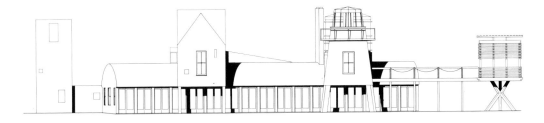

West elevation / Prospetto ovest

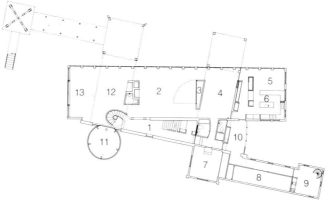

1. Entry hall
2. Living room
3. Painting storage
4. Dining room
5. Breakfast room
6. Kitchen/pantry
7. Media room
8. Storage
9. Apartment
10. Mudroom
11. Green house
12. Den
13. Sunroom

Ground floor plan/ Pianta piano terra

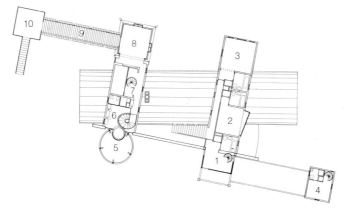

1. Guest suite
2. Guest suite
3. Guest suite
4. Apartment
5. Green house
6. Master bath
7. Dressing area
8. Master bedroom
9. Walkway
10. Gazebo

First floor plan/ Pianta primo piano

THE WHITE COUPLE

Studio Architrope, A. Bishop Bartle & J. Kirschenfeld Architects. Canaan, New York

The building looks like a couple of candid girls sitting on a lawn in silent contemplation, their white dresses standing out against the rich countryside around them, but at the same time harmonizing, blending as in a painting of the Romantic school. Knowingly perched on a large grassy slope overlooking the Hudson River valley, this "twin" home designed for the painter Catherine Mosley, is a country transposition of the urban type of house consisting of two buildings facing across a courtyard. Besides taking this type as their model, the architects have paid careful attention to the American neoclassical tradition, a style that enjoyed a particularly fruitful season in this area with the early colonists of 1840–50. But the choice of this particular form, implanted in the countryside, was also prompted by the long tradition of American college campuses, of which the Charlottesville campus in Virginia (1817) designed by Thomas Jefferson himself, is the chief point of reference. But rather than to this somewhat monumental model, the twin houses on this Canaan hillside seem to refer to the Wigh and Cliosophic Hall at Princeton (1837–38). As in that instance, the design of these two white mirror-like buildings is based on a set of precise architectural elements: the gabled roof, which rises to a fine tympanum; and the high columned porch overlooking the inner court, whose slope provides an excellent vantage point for observing the fine panorama of the valley below. The client's specific request for two separate blocks respectively containing the summer residence and the painting studio has resulted in two units that eschew mere revival in favor of an exacting interpretation of classicizing vocabulary, with the addition of compositional liberties such as the tall windows, terminating on the south front with a grid of wooden panels; and likewise the verandahs on the upper story, which offer a shady respite for the hot summer afternoons. And while the arrangement of the windows on the ground floor, asymmetrical at the side porches and irregularly spaced along the outer sides, may seem overtly uncanonical, conformity is reasserted in the classical symmetry of the tympanums, which are pierced identically by two small square windows in the north face, and by three narrow windows in the south. The general white aura enveloping the buildings is complemented by the metal roofs and the plain wood fittings that continue inside with the floor boards and accentuation of structural detail (beams, pillars, stairs, and verandahs). White is also used for the wall of the rooms, bar those of the glazed verandah overlooking the lawns. Also giving onto the greenery are the south rooms of the studio and living unit, with their full-height windows. While this double house manages to define precise domestic spaces and work areas, and gives an appearance of completeness from the outside, the parallel arrangement of the two buildings allow for future extensions to be built. For the time being, however, the two houses are engaged in an intense dialogue with the landscape around them.

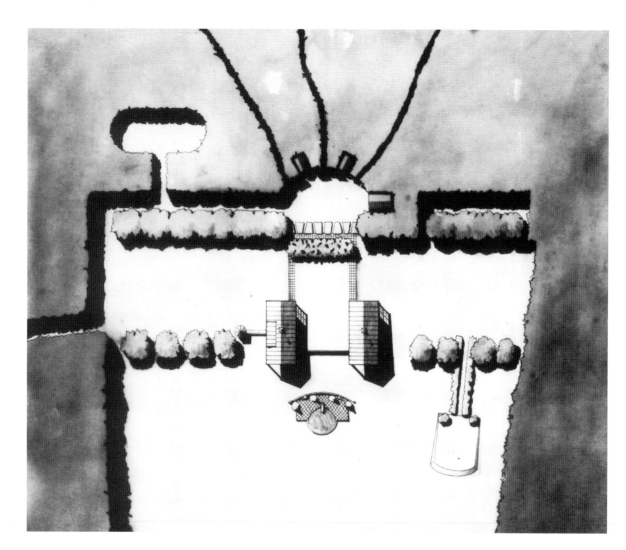

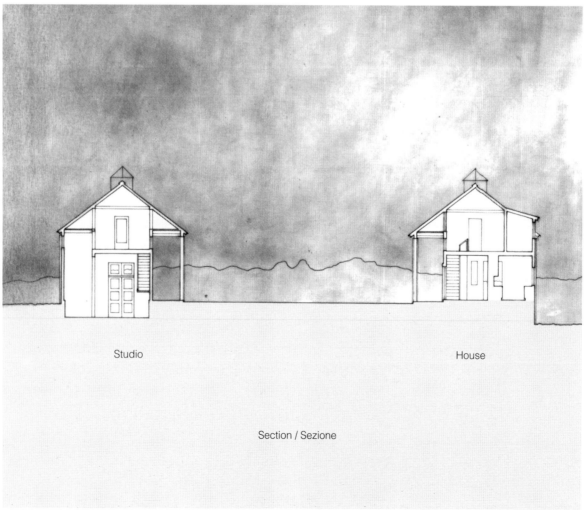

Studio

House

Section / Sezione

Sembrano due eleganti, gentili e candide fanciulle adagiate su un prato in assoluto silenzio, osservano il generoso paesaggio dell'intorno distaccandosene per il bianco del loro vestito, ma allo stesso tempo, in armonia, possono farne parte come in una composizione pittorica dei paesaggisti romantici. Sapientemente isolate sopra un grande pendio erboso affacciato sulla vallata del fiume Hudson, questa coppia di case gemelle progettate per l'artista Catherine Mosley, traducono la tipologia urbana di due edifici affacciati sul cortile interno in chiave paesaggistica. In questo caso i giovani architetti, oltre a ripercorrere questa forma urbana, hanno esaminato con attenzione la migliore tradizione neoclassica americana che proprio in questa zona trovò valide espressioni nell'architettura fondativa dei coloni che vi arrivarono tra il 1840 e il 1850. Ma la scelta di questa precisa morfologia architettonica calata nel verde, come affermano gli stessi autori, proviene anche dalla ricca tradizione dei campus universitari americani di cui il villaggio accademico di Charlottesville in Virginia (1817), progettato dal presidente Thomas Jefferson, costituisce l'esempio principe. Ma più che a quel progetto monumentale e rigoroso le due case gemelle sorte su uno dei prati delle colline di Canaan sembrano rifarsi per dimensione e figura alle *Wigh* e *Cliosophic hall* dell'università di Princeton (1837-38). Come in quel caso, le due bianche costruzioni speculari sono caratterizzate da pochi e precisi elementi architettonici: i tetti a falda, che nelle testate si trasformano in forti timpani regolari, l'alto portico colonnato affacciato sulla corte interna che in questo caso, sfruttando la pendenza del terreno, si trasforma in vero e proprio palcoscenico erboso da cui osservare la valle prospiciente. L'esigenza espressa dalla committenza di avere due corpi separati per la residenza estiva e lo studio di pittura, ha portato alla definizione di due volumi che, lontani da ogni facile revival, rielaborano con rigore alcuni elementi della grammatica classica, aggiungendovi libertà compositive come le ampie vetrate laterali, concluse nei fronti a sud con una griglia quadrata di pannelli di legno. Ma anche come le verande pensili del piano superiore usate per riposare ventilati all'ombra nei pomeriggi estivi. Anche la disposizione delle aperture del piano terreno, asimmetriche nelle testate sotto i portici, e dosate con irregolarità lungo le pareti esterne, appare lontana dalle regole canoniche del classicismo, che viene tuttavia richiamato nella simmetria dei timpani, segnati in modo identico da due piccole finestre quadrate verso nord e da due strette aperture tripartite a sud. Il bianco che avvolge le costruzioni si affianca al metallo delle coperture e al legno naturale che prosegue negli interni a listoni come parte della pavimentazione e come materiale che sottolinea gli elementi strutturali (travi, pilastri, scale e verande sospese). Il bianco copre anche le pareti delle stanze ad esclusione di quelle delle verande vetrate, aperte sul prato sottostante. Verso il verde sono proiettati anche i grandi e alti locali dello studio e della casa nella parti conclusive a sud con le pareti vetrate a tutt'altezza. La doppia casa, se da un lato definisce nel suo interno precisi spazi domestici e di lavoro e se nella figura esterna sottolinea il suo aspetto compiuto, nella disposizione parallela e aperta dei due corpi permette future addizioni. Per ora, come affermano gli autori, "le due case sorgono solitarie in un impegnativo rapporto con il grandioso paesaggio e con la realtà circostante".

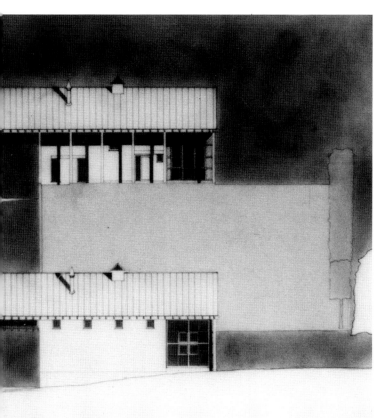

West elevation / Prospetto ovest

East elevation / Prospetto est

COMPOSIZIONE URBANA
URBAN COMPOSITION
Eric Cobb Architect. Seattle, Washington

Set into a gently sloping hillside site, this house, which was built for the architect's parents, lies just ten minutes out of Seattle in a residential area buried in lush woodland. The new home is a light and airy construction composed of a series of meticulously chosen materials whose juxtapositions and combination have been evidently pondered at length. The plan of the building is essentially delineated by two separate paths that both distribute and connect the internal spaces. The two helical courses describe a "guest route," which leads from the outside pavement to the entrance area, rising directly to the main terrace above. This is contrasted by the "domestic route" that runs from the road to the garage, climbs to the kitchen that gives onto the large bright living room, and then crosses its counterpart before disappearing into the bedroom and study overlooking the terrace. As evidenced by the architectural sketches, the two paths describe the layout of the house which, set on two levels with a basement garage, has been carefully eased into the site without altering the tree formation, and with the minimum disturbance of the terrain. The entire construction faces south to take full advantage of the natural light and the fine view of the city. The south front is therefore the main facade, and its design summarizes the entire construction. Markedly horizontal in appearance, the facade is composed of two bands of vertical cedar sidings, alternating with the metal garage vents and a long strip window with an industrial *brise-soleil* marking the upper story, which houses the living room and kitchen. Flanking this partition at the right is the taller construction, extending from the second-story bedroom, corresponding with the little terrace of the living room and kitchen below, where the strip window and corresponding wooden band break back toward the interior, thus augmenting the balcony space and enlivening the pattern of the facade. The complex composition is notable for its airy combination of mass and void, animated by a metal access stairway of steel cables strung from iron uprights. The materials chosen include wood for the facade; aluminum for the window and door frames (glazing has also been employed to lighten the first-floor balcony); stone for the base course of the small terraced garden toward the pavement linked to the pathway; metal grilles used horizontally (as *brises-soleil*) and vertically (for the construction's lightweight plinth that provides ventilation for the basement garage). The clever

variations of surface texture and detailing form a kind of abstract geometric assemblage that makes a clear statement of the design's formal and material composition. The same compositional principles are reiterated in the interiors, which, beyond a covered entrance in the left side of the house at the top of a flight of steps, includes a guest bedroom and bathroom on the left and, centrally, an ample and well-lit living room linked to the kitchen and the lobby from the garage, equipped with a small lift. The kitchen area is screened by a work unit in solid maple, which is also used for the parquet floor. The simple geometry of this piece of furniture between the kitchen and living room is endorsed by a customized unit flanking a slanting wall that encloses a small wooden and metal stairway leading to the second level. Arranged on two sides of the large terrace above, which affords a completely private sun deck, is the master bedroom and a small study that doubles up as a guest bedroom.

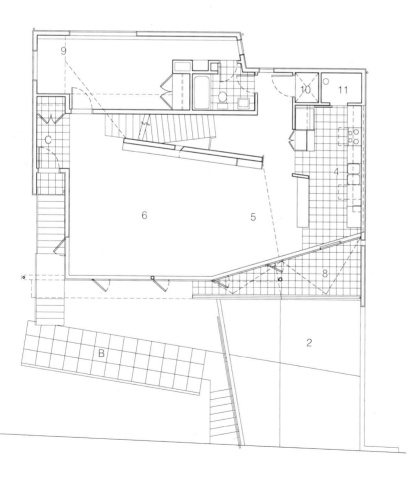

GUEST PATH
A. Sidewalk
B. Approach
C. Entry stair
D. Roof deck / garden

DOMESTIC PATH
1. Street
2. Driveway
3. Carport stair
4. Kitchen
5. Dining
6. Living stair
7. Bedroom

SPURS / LOOPS
8. Terrace
9. Study / guestroom
10. Elevator
11. Pantry / Laundry
12. Studio / Guestroom

First floor / Primo piano

Second floor / Secondo piano

Una casa costruita per i propri genitori a dieci minuti dal centro di Seattle, in una zona residenziale ricca di verde e caratterizzata per l'andamento in pendenza del terreno dovuto alla morfologia collinare del luogo. Pensata come costruzione leggera, composta da una serie di precisi materiali scelti e denunciati con chiarezza e sincerità costruttiva nel loro accostamento figurativo e nelle scelte compositive generali, la casa si propone come studiata organizzazione spaziale scandita essenzialmente da due differenti percorsi, che distribuiscono e connettono gli spazi interni. I due tragitti elicoidali di riferimento si dividono in un "percorso per gli ospiti", che dal marciapiede prospiciente si spinge verso la zona ingresso per poi salire direttamente alla grande terrazza di copertura e nel più complesso "percorso domestico", che dalla strada arriva al garage, sale nella cucina aperta verso il luminoso soggiorno, per poi salire, intersecandosi con il primo, verso la camera da letto e lo studio affacciati sull'ampia terrazza. Come viene evidenziato dai diagrammi di studio, i due percorsi determinano gli spazi della casa che, sviluppata su due livelli, più il seminterrato del garage, è stata inserita nel lotto senza alterare la situazione arborea esistente e con il minimo scavo nel terreno della collina. L'intera costruzione è rivolta verso sud, per sfruttare nel migliore dei modi la luce naturale e per offrire la migliore vista della città. É quindi il lato sud a proporsi come fronte principale e come sintesi compositiva dell'intera costruzione. Caratterizzata da un andamento orizzontale, la facciata è composta da due strisce rivestite in legno di cedro a listelli verticali, alternate alla griglia metallica di areazione per il garage e alla lunga finestra a nastro con brise soleil in rete metallica industriale che segnano lo spazio del primo piano, dove sono ubicati soggiorno e cucina. A questa partizione si affianca sulla destra il volume più alto e in aggetto della camera da letto del secondo livello, cui

corrisponde il piccolo terrazzo sottostante di soggiorno e cucina, dove la finestra a nastro e la fascia lignea corrispondente si arretrano verso l'interno permettendo così di ampliare lo spazio del balcone e arricchendo allo stesso tempo il disegno di facciata. La complessa composizione si caratterizza per la leggerezza dello studiato accostamento tra pieni e vuoti, delle scale metalliche di accesso con ringhiere in ferro e cavi di acciaio. I materiali scelti sono il legno per le facciate, l'alluminio per gli infissi, le trasparenze del vetro impiegato anche per alleggerire la raffinata balaustra del balcone al primo piano, la pietra per il basamento del piccolo giardino verso il marciapiede connesso al percorso d'ingresso, le reti metalliche in orizzontale (il brise soleil) e in verticale (l'etereo zoccolo della costruzione costituito dalle aperture di aerazione dei box): una serie di variazioni di superfici e di dettagli pensati anche come assemblaggio geometrico astratto ed esposti inequivocabilmente per la loro qualità formale e per la loro struttura materica. Gli stessi principi compositivi si ritrovano anche nell'interno che, dopo l'ingresso coperto, ricavato sul lato sinistro della casa e raggiungibile con una scala , propone sulla sinistra una camera per gli ospiti con bagno proprio e di fronte l'ampio e luminoso soggiorno connesso alla cucina e alla zona di arrivo dal garage, in cui è ubicato anche il piccolo ascensore. La zona cucina è schermata da un mobile di lavoro in legno d'acero, materiale impiegato anche per i parquet della pavimentazione. Alla geometria elementare del mobile-filtro tra cucina e soggiorno corrisponde la figura di quello su disegno affiancato alla parete inclinata che nasconde la leggera scala in legno e metallo di salita al secondo livello. Qui, intorno al grande terrazzo di copertura, vero e proprio solarium protetto e appartato, si sviluppano su due lati la camera da letto padronale e uno studio/camera per gli ospiti.

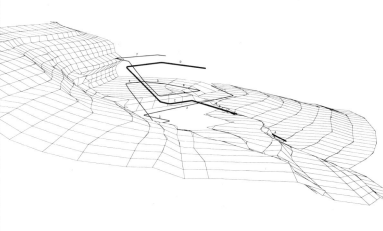

Path diagram / Diagramma

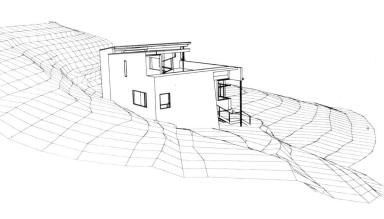

West elevation / Prospetto ovest

Section looking east / Sezione est

41

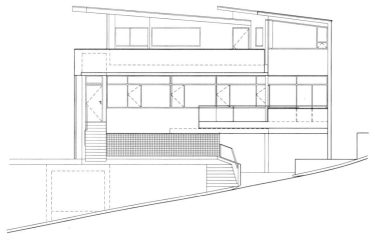

South elevation / Prospetto sud

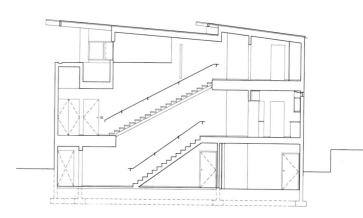

Section looking north / Sezione nord

MULTIPLE COTTAGE

David Coleman Architect. Lake Seymore, Vermont

In its American form, the traditional English-style country cottage has undergone a complex evolution that is closely tied to the formation of the nation. In the 1800s the cottage was the standard type of dwelling the European colonists built with their own hands on their farm plot. This widespread type of building did not require an architect and was therefore a popular form of "self-building" that became common for houses by the lakeside or in the woods. Even today the cottage format is a staple of traditional Anglo-Saxon architecture, the cozy one- or two-story timber and stone house with gabled roof, a simple and reassuring kind of dwelling. A variegated building type which in America has drawn on timeworn building techniques and categories for over a century. The project for this weekend home tastefully slotted into the woodland by Lake Seymore takes its cue directly from the cottage tradition, recasting certain features in a novel creative mode. Built on the hillside sloping down toward the water, slightly raised from the ground on a timber plinth, this modern multiple cottage is a grouping of three distinct units extend toward the water, set in a tiered formation to create

44

external spaces that underline the rapport between construction and natural setting. The two main units on a rectangular plan, lying slightly skewed, with gabled roofs, vertical plank facades painted brick red and punctuated by small windows alternating with large fully glazed sections, are propped on a gray timber structure forming a series of firewood storage spaces in the interstices between floor and sloping terrain. Between the two cottages stands a smaller unit providing linkage; on the lake front it offers a bright and airy patio with wide windows contained within a strict geometrical framework. The patio is flanked by two wooden stairways that make their way through the narrow gap between the building units down to the grassy slope. This living space, a little study, and a second informal living room, is set on the loggia connecting the two skewed cottage units; uphill it allows for a small irregularly shaped court accessed from the road, like a small enclosed patio, an outdoor extension of the house's interiors. The exterior facing of the two cottages corresponds to the different functions each contains. The one placed parallel to the porch has a plain frontage cut with small vertical windows, and houses the night area with the master bedroom facing the lake, and the two children's bedrooms separated by walk-through closets and a shared bathroom. This looks onto the loggia which, besides bridging the two main units, acts as a filter between the little court above and the central patio. This connectivity is further underscored by the materials used for the flooring, local green slate, which extends into the kitchen and bathroom, offsetting the pine parquet that covers the rest of the floor. The skewed cottage contains all the day functions around a large single split-level space that accommodates the slope of the terrain, marking off living room from dining area, and kitchen, which is tucked behind the large centrally placed fireplace that rises to the ceiling, constructed in small blocks of gray stone. The large windows on three sides of the living room offer a superb panorama of the lake, and provide generous natural lighting for the entire day area, together with the skylights over the dining room.

Landscape plan / Pianta del paesaggio

Il cottage, abitazione rustica di campagna di origine inglese, ha conosciuto in America una storia complessa che ha legato questa espressione abitativa alla storia della formazione della Nazione. Il cottage fu infatti nell'Ottocento l'abitazione dei coloni, quella che ogni europeo si costruiva con le proprie mani accanto ai campi da coltivare.

Questa diffusa tipologia, 'architettura senza architetto', frutto di autocostruzione ed espressione popolare, divenne poi il riferimento per le residenze estive costruite in prossimità dei laghi e all'interno dei boschi. Il cottage permane così a tutt'oggi un elemento tipico di tutta l'architettura anglosassone, piccola casa in legno e pietra a uno o due piani con tetto a falda più o meno spiovente, confortevole e dall'immagine elementare e rassicurante. Una variegata tipologia che dai secoli scorsi ripete in America tecniche costruttive e figure architettoniche sedimentate nella memoria collettiva. Il progetto di questa casa per week-end, calata con garbo nel bosco in riva al lago Seymore, si collega direttamente a questa ricca tradizione rivisitandone e rileggendone con creatività le figure di riferimento.

Costruito sul terreno digradante verso il lago, staccato in parte dal terreno tramite la struttura in legno a vista di sostegno, questo moderno cottage multiplo si propone come somma di tre corpi distinti protesi verso il lago e affiancati in modo digradante per formare degli spazi esterni che sottolineano il rapporto tra la costruzione e la natura all'intorno. I due corpi principali a pianta rettangolare, regolari, ma disassati, con tetti a falda, facciate di legno a doghe verticali dipinte di rosso mattone movimentate da piccole finestre e generose vetrate, sono sostenuti dalla struttura lignea grigia a vista che forma negli spazi liberi tra pavimento e terreno scosceso dei vani per depositare la legna.

Tra i due cottage è posizionato un corpo minore centrale, cerniera compositiva che verso il lago si propone come luminoso portico coperto, con ampie vetrate poste all'interno della rigorosa geometria strutturale. Il portico è affiancato lateralmente da due scalette di legno che, innestate negli stretti spazi liberi di risulta tra i tre volumi affiancati, scendono verso il prato in pendio. Questo spazio abitativo, piccolo studio e ulteriore informale soggiorno, si innesta sulla loggia distributiva che connette i due cottage disassati e a monte lascia libera una piccola corte irregolare di accesso dalla strada, sorta di piccolo patio protetto, pensato come spazio della casa all'aria aperta.

Al diverso trattamento di facciata dei due cottage corrispondono le differenti funzioni interne; quello posto in parallelo al portico, dalle facciate più piene e segnate da piccole finestre rettangolari verticali, ospita la zona notte con la stanza da letto padronale rivolta verso il lago e due camere da letto per i bambini separate da funzionali cabine armadio e con un unico bagno in comune. Questo è rivolto verso la loggia che, oltre a collegare i due corpi principali, si pone anche come elemento filtro tra corte a monte e portico centrale. Il carattere di elemento connettivo è sottolineato anche dal materiale della pavimentazione: in ardesia verde locale che si estende nella cucina e nel bagno distaccandosi dai parquet di abete impiegati per il resto delle superfici. Nel cottage disassato è organizzata l'intera zona giorno in un grande spazio unitario caratterizzato dall'andamento a diverse quote del pavimento che, seguendo il pendio del terreno, definisce le zone del soggiorno, della sala da pranzo e della cucina. Quest'ultima è nascosta alle spalle del grande camino centrale a tutt'altezza, costruito in blocchetti grigi refrattari. Le grandi vetrate ben ripartite dei tre lati del soggiorno offrono una splendida vista del lago oltre a illuminare con generosità l'intera zona giorno insieme ai lucernari posti sopra la sala da pranzo.

East elevation / Prospetto est

Ground floor / Piano terra

1. courtyard
2. loggia
3. porch
4. kitchen
5. dining room
6. living room
7. master bedroom
8. hall
9. childrens bedrooms

Section / Sezione

50

LA GRIGLIA NEL BOSCO
A GRID IN THE WOOD

Peter Forbes and Associates Inc. Mount Desert Island, Maine

A house in the woods, a place to observe the surrounding nature, constructed in inert, antiallergenic materials such as steel and aluminum, with especially cultivated wood (untreated cedar for the floors), and with the exclusion of formaldehyde, polycarbons, and polyurethane, in strict compliance with the client's brief. These were the points of departure for designing a house in the woods, a project that turned out to be a progressive experiment in healthy ecological construction, a comfortable place open to the countryside without forgoing its formal identity and strong compositional character. Unlike bioarchitecture, which tends to forgo a concerted design and instead wrap up the architecture in vegetation and replace the roof with solar panels, this house built in the depths of a dense wood has an unmistakable architectural persona that takes its cue from the gabled cottage-type but progressively interrupts the gabled profile, reworking the facades and the layout of the interiors. The house has three stories contained in a single unitary space under the tall gable, which is clad in aluminum and interrupted at the crown by the bathroom and elevator housing. The interior is a complex unitary space open toward the roof, and characterized by a close-knit grid structure made of square steel tubing painted white that configures the space while forming the support framework for each story. The large house grid, which contains an assortment of different compositional and functional units – such as the white kitchen and the slender sloping stairway on the ground story, the spiral stairway leading to the first and second stories, and the glazed elevator encased in a red metal structure – is directly complemented by the solution adopted for the facade. The two main sides are set with large regular windows on a square grid which, in correspondence with the structural grid inside, divide into four equal parts the reference module, defining the two main facades of the house as glazed walls that rise to the roof and terminate level with the solid timber-clad part of the back wall in which the service facilities are located. The large roof develops in two halves of different dimensions; the front slope rises to a lower height than the back slope, ending in a lower building section with a flat roof from which, either side of the main central chimney in reinforced concrete and stone, extends a covered terrace and a small atrium linked to the lawn beyond via a set of stone steps arranged symmetrically. All the spaces are interconnecting, and the night zones of the first and second floors are also facing the ground-floor living space. The only exceptions are the bathrooms and closets, which are separated by the main unitary space. The overall impression is of an open refuge in the woods filled with colors and light, filtered through the ample band of windows, while from the windows on the last story, in the block suspended over the roof in a kind of belvedere extending into the horizon, one can see the distant mountains of Acadia National Park.

Una casa nel bosco per osservare la natura che l'avvolge, costruita con materiali antiallergici e inerti come l'acciaio e l'alluminio, con essenze lignee coltivate (il legno di cedro non trattato impiegato per i pavimenti) e con grande attenzione a non impiegare formaldeide, policarbonati e poliuretano, su specifica richiesta della committenza. Questi i punti di partenza per progettare una casa nel verde che si è via via definita come una riuscita sperimentazione di costruzione ecologica e salubre, confortevole e aperta verso il paesaggio, senza rinunciare alla propria identità formale e a un forte carattere compositivo. A differenza della bioarchitettura che in nome dell'uso di materiali naturali e di energie alternative il più delle volte sacrifica il progetto nascondendo l'architettura sotto la vegetazione e sostituendo al tetto una batteria di pannelli solari, questa casa costruita in mezzo a un fitto bosco si propone come un segno abitabile preciso e inequivocabile che trova nel riferimento del cottage a doppia falda il suo spunto iniziale per poi sviluppare questa tipologia di base rompendone i profili, reinventando il disegno delle facciate e la distribuzione degli spazi interni. La casa si sviluppa su tre piani contenuti in un unico spazio unitario sotto l'alta falda del tetto rivestito di alluminio interrotto sulla sommità dal volume dei bagni e dell'arrivo dell'ascensore. L'interno si propone così come complesso ambiente unitario aperto verso l'alto e caratterizzato dalla fitta struttura a griglia regolare formata da tubi di acciaio a sezione quadrata tinteggiati di bianco che disegnano lo spazio sostenendo i vari livelli. La grande griglia della casa, in cui si intrecciano e si distribuiscono sog-

Foundation plan
Piano delle fondazioni

Ground level plan
Pianta piano terreno

First level plan
Pianta del primo piano

Dormer plan
Abbaino

getti compositivi e funzionali come il banco cucina attrezzato e la leggera scala di lamiera inclinata del piano terreno, quella a chiocciola che porta al primo e al secondo livello e l'ascensore di cristallo ingabbiato da una struttura metallica rossa, trova nelle soluzioni di facciata il suo diretto elemento complementare. I due lati maggiori si caratterizzano per le grandi vetrate a maglia quadrata regolare che in corrispondenza della griglia strutturale interna dividono in quattro parti uguali il modulo di riferimento definendo le due grandi facciate della casa come pareti vetrate continue regolari che raggiungono il tetto e si fermano in corrispondenza della parte piena rivestita in legno del retro della casa, in cui è ubicata la zona servizi. La grande copertura si sviluppa secondo due falde a diversa dimensione; quella verso il fronte si spinge a una quota inferiore di quella del retro per trovare come appoggio conclusivo un volume basso con copertura piana dove sono disposti, ai lati del grande camino centrale in cemento armato e pietra, un terrazzo coperto e un piccolo atrio collegati al prato circostante con una serie di gradini in pietra disposti in modo simmetrico. Tutti gli spazi sono collegati tra loro, anche le zone notte del primo e secondo piano sono affacciate sul soggiorno del piano terreno. Unica eccezione sono i bagni e i ripostigli separati dal grande spazio unitario. Un'architettura che si propone come aperto rifugio nel verde riempito dai colori e dalla luce del paesaggio filtrati dalle grandi e luminose vetrate continue, mentre dalle finestre dell'ultimo livello, nel volume sospeso sopra la grande copertura, sorta di belvedere proteso verso l'orizzonte, si osservano in lontananza le montagne dell'Acadia Park.

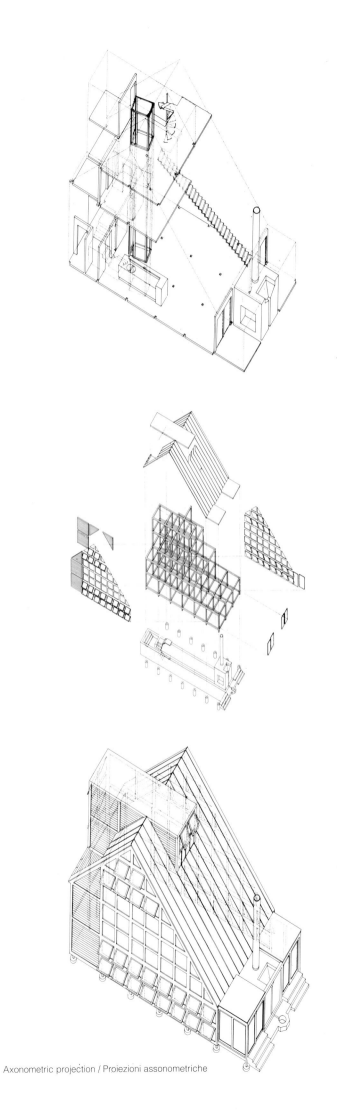

59

Axonometric projection / Proiezioni assonometriche

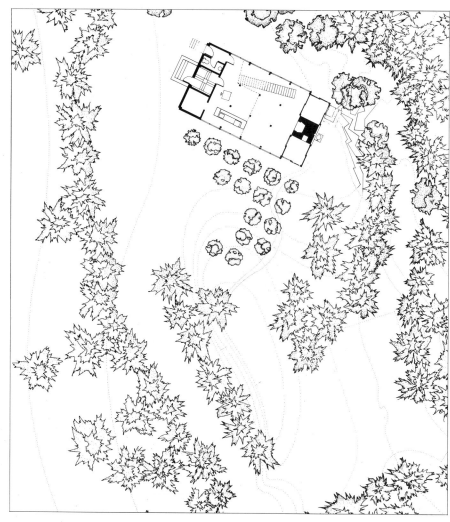

64

An appealing landscape of level plains and gentle wooded hillside – the ideal backdrop for an

example of rural vernacular architecture – is the setting for this holiday home, obtained by the conversion and enlargement of a farmstead. Together with the two grain silos alongside, the preexisting structure, a traditional two-story building clad in white weatherboard with a gabled roof and broad verandah on three sides, stands out prominently in this flat landscape. The traditional rural architecture has been respected as a hallmark of farming activity and of man's presence on the land, and even endorsed by the new enlargement scheme. This required a new living room, wall space for the picture collection, a large bedroom, and an indoor swimming pool. The cues for the new layout were taken primarily from the landscape, in the successful attempt to maintain the preexisting architecture as the principal points of reference for both volumes and shapes, particularly as regards dimensions, and

the overall regard for integration with the site. The extension is conceived as a careful annexing of elements that pays homage to the host architecture while avoiding a revival approach and looking confidently modern. Four different domestic shapes are developed on a single story below that of the original house; these are characterized by four differently styled roofs corresponding to the new functions within. The roofs of the silos are composed of joined copper sheeting, making an interesting contrast with the site and an echo of rural tradition. The first new unit flanks the lower section linked to the old house is the large living room, with its gabled roof and detailed ceiling beams that offer a striking sculptural and volumetric feature, complemented by the handsome stone fireplace that fills an entire wall. The master bedroom is tucked under a depressed barrel vault that echoes the lower one that underscores the long and narrow pool, which is denoted on one side by a series of trunk-columns disguising the structural pillars, and on the other by a double band of windows. This, together with the main window, gives onto the land-scape, while the pool ends in a stone wall, offering visual linkage between inside and out, into which a statue (*Joy of the Waters*, by Harriet Frishmuth) is set, as in the famous Mies van der Rohe pavilion in Barcelona. The rectangular space with flat roof delegated for the picture gallery separates the bedroom and living room from the swimming pool, affording an accessory entrance that is denoted by the lowered floor area around the pool, like a sunken garden, to allow for sunbathing during the summer months without extra visual barriers to ensure privacy. Two tall yellow hearths alternate with stretches of undressed masonry, large windows, and sophisticated sections of walls consisting of plaster and stucco panels set in metal gridwork, and with horizontal boards, creating an architecture that is refined, modern, and respectful of the landscape and history of the place.

In un paesaggio agreste di largo respiro caratterizzato da una grande distesa pianeggiante e da dolci colline alberate, perfetta cornice per inquadrare una scena dell'architettura rurale vernacolare americana, sorge questo progetto per una casa di vacanze, ampliamento di un insediamento agricolo. La casa preesistente, in doghe di legno bianche orizzontali, sviluppata su due piani sotto un tetto a falda, circondata su tre lati da una generosa veranda, si presenta, insieme ai silos bianchi che l'affiancano, come forte segno emergente nel paesaggio pianeggiante. Segnale di attività agricola e di presenza umana nella natura, l'insieme delle tradizionali costruzioni rurali è stato assunto come punto fermo, testimonianza non solo architettonica da mantenere e valorizzare tramite il nuovo progetto di ampliamento. Questo richiedeva un nuovo soggiorno, uno spazio per collocare una collezione di quadri, una

fronto con il sito e di richiamo alla tradizione rurale. Il primo spazio che si incontra a fianco del corpo basso di collegamento alla vecchia casa è il grande soggiorno con copertura a falda che nell'interno denuncia la struttura di legno delle travi di copertura pensate anche come efficace presenza scultorea e volumetrica insieme al forte camino di pietra che segna un'intera parete. La camera da letto padronale è invece contenuta sotto una volta a botte ribassata che riprende quella inferiore chiamata a sottolineare la lunga e stretta piscina segnata su un lato da una serie di colonne-tronchi che rivestono i pilastri in ferro strutturali e sull'altro da una doppia finestra a nastro continuo. Questa, insieme alla grande vetrata principale, apre verso il paesaggio la vasca natatoria conclusa da una parete in pietra, elemento di raccordo tra interno ed esterno, su cui si staglia, come nel famoso padiglione di Mies van der Rohe a

grande camera da letto e una piscina coperta. Le scelte compositive del nuovo intervento sono state anzitutto di tipo paesaggistico, nel riuscito tentativo di mantenere le preesistenze architettoniche come soggetti primari, volumi e figure di riferimento, soprattutto dal punto di vista dimensionale e nell'attenzione complessiva rivolta all'inserimento nel contesto. L'ampliamento si propone come studiata annessione che rifiutando la logica dei revivals stilistici, non rinuncia a sottili richiami con le architetture con cui si confronta, mantenendo tuttavia con convinzione la propria modernità. Quattro forme abitative sviluppate su un solo livello, inferiore a quello della vecchia casa, sono caratterizzate da altrettante figure di copertura corrispondenti alle nuove funzioni interne. I tetti in lamiera di rame a pannelli congiunti rivisitano apertamente quelli a cupola dei silos esistenti costituendo un valido elemento di con-

Barcellona, una statua femminile ("Joy of the Waters" di Harriet Frishmuth). Lo spazio rettangolare con copertura piana dedicato all'esposizione dei quadri separa camera da letto e soggiorno dalla piscina, configurandosi anche come nuovo ingresso, raccordato alla zona pavimentata ribassata di fronte alla piscina: sorta di piccolo giardino costruito a quota inferiore rispetto al terreno all'intorno, per permetterne l'uso a solarium nei mesi estivi senza l'ausilio di barriere visive verticali di garanzia alla necessaria privacy. Due alti camini intonacati di giallo si alternano a campiture in muratura, ad ampie vetrate e a raffinate pareti composte da parti intonacate, da pannelli in stucco contenuti in precise maglie metalliche, da fasce orizzontali di rivestimento ligneo, per definire un'architettura complessa e raffinata, moderna e rispettosa, rapportata al paesaggio e alla storia del luogo.

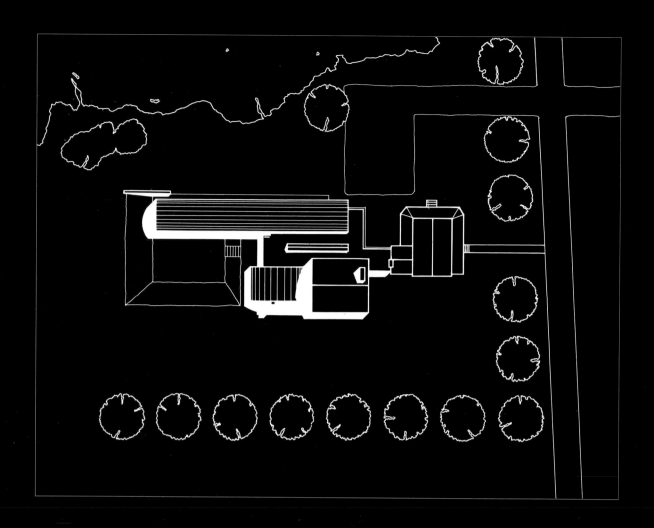

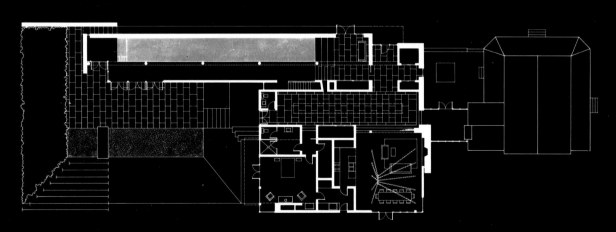

Plan / Pianta

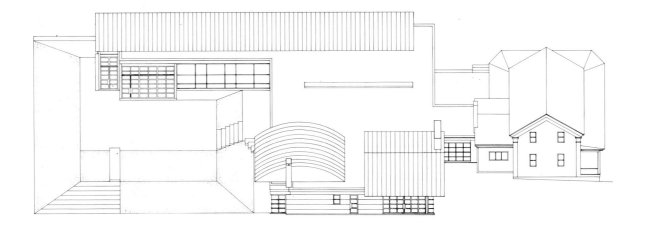

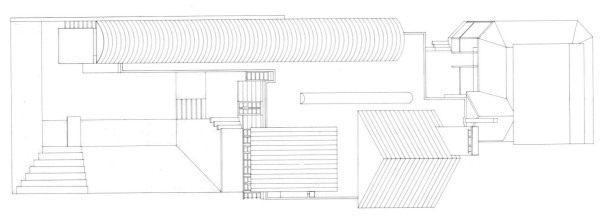

LA CASA PONTE
BRIDGE HOUSE
Peter L. Gluck Architect. Olive Bridge, New York

This holiday home built in a clearing in the woodlands of Olive Bridge stands as an unabashed landmark in the landscape, a complex living volume that is conceived above all as an intersection of paths and directions applied to place and context – a kind of domestic bridge that projects its different facets toward the variegated natural surroundings, complying with the diversity of the terrain. Apart from serving as an architectural model for the building type itself, the "bridge" concept plays a symbolic role also: the house is basically a persuasive reworking of rural architecture of the past, and in this sense forms a bridge to the present, a strong link with the American farmland, while eschewing mere stylistic revivalism. The house consists in the architectural union of three shapes that can be easily identified in formal terms and for the adroit mixture of materials. One section is distributed on three levels, comprised of a union of two distinct forms grafted with a horizontal domestic space suspended on slender iron pillars: a bridge amid the greenery. The main block is a living cube clad in rectangular panels of concrete forming an imposing portal-facade that shows deference to the rigorous proportions of American neo-Palladianism, a style adopted for monumental architecture and public buildings reapplied to the country villas of wealthy landown-

ers. The affirmative statement is offered in the prospect looking out over the lawns, and is pierced by large central windows. Inside, a strict geometry governs the full-height lobby onto which the three levels of the secondary section face, which is devised as a smaller rural building of wooden sidings and metal roof. Here in the tight interlocking of these two neatly defined elements – which are furthermore grafted with a suspended bridge section contain-ing the bedrooms of the night zone – are lodged the public parts of the house; the spacious and well-lit dou-ble-height space accommodates the living and dining rooms, which are projected toward the thick woods outside via the large windows framed in mahogany composed in horizontal rectangular panels. A broad fire-place is set into the middle of one of the win-dows, carefully dovetailed with the pattern of the frame. Wood is also used for the beams of the roof, which carries a terrace, and for the floors, in strips of yellow birch. In the day area, the junction of the two three-story sections is resolved via a facade pierced with square aper-tures of varying dimensions, and by a complex system of metal stairways and catwalks that define the various parts of the timber-clad house. At ground-floor level the kitchen, which gives onto the living and dining area, is characterized by a structural trunk in plain timber that extends all the way to the top and props up the beams supporting the neighboring terrace. The intermediate story houses the library, billiard room, and a small study; the upper story, cradled beneath the sloping roof, provides access to the external walkway. The part of the house that accommodates the night zones is the bridge section, clad in aluminum panels of the kind traditionally used in American rural building early this century. The string of bedrooms give onto a long and bright corridor with a continuous window. The rooms themselves are divided by a series of independent bathrooms. The frontage of the night zone looking out onto the wood side is cut with square windows of two distinct sizes, carefully arranged to look haphazard. The bridge to the night zone, propped on a series of red metal posts, is the private, exclusive section of the house, and emerges from the junction at the first level of the timber section of the building, terminating in the master bedroom, which is distinguished visually by its vaulted sheet-metal roof. From here another catwalk, affording a further note of visual punctuation, extends toward the wood with a small stair linked to the pathway leading from the parking lot, which is ensconced in the wood out of sight of the house.

Questa casa per le vacanze costruita in una radura del bosco di Olive Bridge si configura come sicuro segno nel paesaggio, complesso volume abitabile pensato anzitutto come incrocio di percorsi e direzioni rapportati al luogo e alla natura dell'intorno. Una sorta di

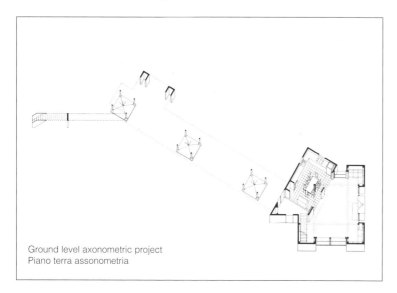

Ground level axonometric project
Piano terra assonometria

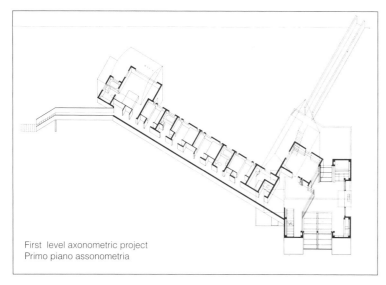

First level axonometric project
Primo piano assonometria

ponte domestico che proietta le sue diverse parti verso la natura e connette i differenti luoghi che la circondano, seguendo e rispettando la movimentata orografia del terreno. Il concetto di ponte, oltre che come figura architettonica e tipologia assunta quale riferimento

compositivo principale, è anche da intendere per il suo valore simbolico; la casa è infatti una sorta di creativa e riuscita rilettura di precisi linguaggi dell'architettura rurale americana e in questo senso definisce anche un 'ponte', un forte legame, con il passato delle forme costruite e dei segni antropici del paesaggio agricolo degli Stati Uniti, rifiutando però apertamente la logica dei facili revivals stilistici. La casa consiste nell'unione architettonica di tre forme ben identificabili sia per riferimenti formali, sia per l'alternarsi nell'impiego di diversi materiali: un volume a tre livelli composto dall'unione di due figure distinte in cui si innesta uno spazio domestico orizzontale sospeso su sottili pilastrini in ferro: il ponte nel verde. Il volume principale è un cubo abitabile rivestito con pannelli rettangolari di cemento chiamati a disegnare una facciata-portale, rigorosa e imponente, che vuole rivisitare la tradizione dei rapporti geometrici e delle proporzioni propri al neopalladianesimo americano, che nell'Ottocento veniva assunto quale linguaggio monumentale e rappresentativo per caratterizzare le ville di campagna dei proprietari terrieri e dei coloni più facoltosi. Questo forte segno architettonico costituisce la facciata della casa rivolta verso la prospettiva aperta del prato, segnata da grandi vetrate centrali. All'interno il rigoroso volume geometrico offre uno spazio a tutt'altezza su cui si rivolgono i tre livelli del secondo corpo della casa, pensato come piccola costruzione di campagna dalle facciate rivestite in doghe di legno e copertura a falda in metallo. Nel forte incastro volumetrico e spaziale dei due elementi così definiti, in cui si innesta anche il ponte sospeso che ospita le numerose camere della zona notte, è organizzata la parte pubblica della casa; il grande e luminoso spazio a tutt'altezza ospita soggiorno e zona pranzo, proiettati verso il verde del bosco tramite le ampie vetrate con infissi in legno di mogano composti secondo pannelli rettangolari orizzontali. Un grande camino interrompe centralmente una delle vetrate, inserendosi con calibrata dimensione all'interno della trama dell'infisso. Il legno è impiegato anche per le travi della copertura su cui è ricavata una terrazza e per il pavimento a listoni di betulla gialla. Nella zona giorno l'innesto tra i due volumi a tre livelli è risolto con una facciata segnata da aperture quadrate di diversa dimensione e da un complesso sistema di scale e passerelle metalliche che scandiscono le diverse funzioni della parte della casa rivestita in legno. Al piano terreno la cucina, aperta verso soggiorno e zona pranzo, è caratterizzata da un tronco strutturale di legno naturale che si sviluppa sino alla sommità come appoggio per l'incrocio delle travi di sostegno della terrazza adiacente. Nel piano intermedio sono ospitate libreria, sala per il biliardo e un piccolo studio, mentre il piano più alto, sotto la ripida copertura a falda, costituisce l'ingresso dalla passerella di legno esterna. La parte della casa che ospita la zona notte è il ponte abitabile rivestito con pannelli di alluminio zigrinato che richiamano il materiale impiegato tradizionalmente nelle costruzioni agricole statunitensi del ventesimo secolo. La serie di camere da letto si affaccia su un lungo e luminoso corridoio segnato da una finestra a nastro continuo. Le stanze sono separate tra loro da una serie di bagni indipendenti. La facciata della zona notte rivolta verso il bosco è invece caratterizzata da una serie di aperture quadrate, a due diverse dimensioni, disposte secondo uno studiato schema apparentemente irregolare. Il ponte della zona notte, sostenuto da una serie di pilastrini in ferro colorati di rosso, costituisce la parte privata e riservata della casa e si sviluppa dall'incastro con il primo livello della porzione lignea della costruzione, per trovare la propria conclusione architettonica nella camera da letto padronale, caratterizzata da una copertura a volta con tetto di lamiera. Da qui una passerella, pensata come ulteriore forte segno conclusivo, si protende verso il bosco con una scala raccordata al sentiero che conduce al parcheggio delle auto, nascosto nel verde e lontano dalla casa.

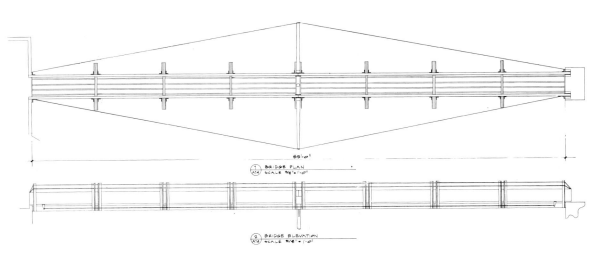

85'-0"

1 BRIDGE PLAN
SCALE 3/8" = 1'-0"

2 BRIDGE ELEVATION
SCALE 3/8" = 1'-0"

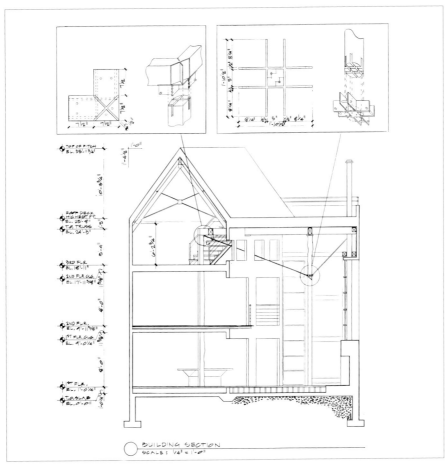

BUILDING SECTION
SCALE: 1/4" = 1'-0"

AMPLIAMENTO LINEARE
LINEAR EXTENSION

Peter L. Gluck Architect. Millerton, New York

This extension scheme to a traditional country house built in the early 1900s evinces a design procedure of signal formal rigor and compositional methodology. The existing construction, a classic timber house with gabled roof and unpretentious weatherboard facade painted white, front verandah, and lower sections interrupting the perimeter of the central unit, was taken as the self-sufficient basis upon which to devise the extension, in deference to building's tradition and rural history. The new building has been gently crafted with the old house so as not to disturb its shape and dimensions, dovetailing the new with the lower existing unit of the building. The original house remains, therefore, the architectural and volumetric pivot of the new extension, which projects toward the little lake nearby. The new building, slightly shorter than the original and visually quite different, is a long linear construction with a regular pattern of mahogany-framed windows alternating with panels of steel. A modern reappraisal of traditional farm architecture, of the barns and sheds that populate the American countryside, the extension contains two stories that develop beneath a steel-clad gabled roof; steel is also used for the stairs inside, for the long first-story balcony, and the lightweight railings of steel cable strung between vertical struts. The sense of extension toward the lake is further stressed by the overall horizontal look of the building expressed in the long narrow extension, but also in the mesh of railings and windows along the facades. The junction point with the old building has spawned a patio over the ample ground-floor kitchen, which provides spatial linkage between the two parts of the building. The same open porch device, this time double-height, returns at the opposite end of the house in the facade looking toward the lake, where the construction merges with the terrain by means of a tiered base course in local stone. At ground-floor level a marquee protects the entranceway, which is paved in the same stone as the steps, a transition space directed toward the rear porch carved out beneath the steel balcony, onto which looks the ample living room with its floor of Douglas fir. In the outside area paved in stone, scooped into the slope of the land is a bedroom, complete with bathroom, and a walk-through closet. Running between the entrance and the kitchen is a double-height space containing the staircase leading to the upper floor. Here are suspended walkway links the rooms to the patio. A spacious study precedes the entrance to the main bedroom, with bathroom, and closet areas, which looks out onto the porch beneath the solid timber projection of the roof.

Questo progetto di ampliamento di una casa di campagna tradizionale dei primi decenni del secolo delinea un procedimento progettuale per rigore formale e metodologia compositiva. La costruzione
esistente, una classica casa in legno con tetto a falda dalle rassicu-
ranti facciate a doghe orizzontali dipinte di bianco, segnata da una
veranda sul fronte principale e con volumi più bassi che spezzano
il perimetro del corpo regolare, è stata assunta come elemento di
partenza e come soggetto compiuto, architettura da valorizzare
come presistenza e traccia di un passato agreste. La nuova costruzione si innesta con leggerezza e attenzione compositiva su quella
precedente senza alterarne figura e dimensioni, impostando lo studiato incastro di annessione sul corpo basso laterale esistente. La
vecchia casa diviene così il volume di riferimento, la testata architettonica e volumetrica del nuovo progetto che si proietta verso il
piccolo lago poco distante. Il nuovo edificio, leggermente più
basso di quello precedente e dall'immagine totalmente differente,
si caratterizza come lunga costruzione lineare dalle vetrate scandi-
te da una maglia regolare di infissi di legno di mogano ad orditura
orizzontale alternati a pannelli di acciaio. Sorta di moderna e riuscita rilettura delle tradizionali costruzioni agricole, dei granai e dei
capannoni che caratterizzano il paesaggio delle campagne americane, l'annessione architettonica sviluppa due livelli sotto una
copertura a falda rivestita con pannelli di acciaio, materiale impiegato anche per la scala interna, il lungo balcone del primo piano e
le leggere ringhiere formate da cavi tesi fra montanti verticali. La
scelta della spinta paesaggistica verso il lago è sottolineata anzitutto dall'andamento orizzontale complessivo della costruzione, sotte-
so nella forma stretta e lunga del corpo di ampliamento, ma anche
dalle orditure delle ringhiere e dalle finestre che disegnano le facciate. L'innesto con la vecchia casa crea un nuovo terrazzo coperto
ricavato sopra l'ampia cucina del piano terreno che funge da cerniera spaziale tra i due corpi architettonici. La stessa soluzione a
portico aperto, però a doppia altezza, si ritrova all'estremità oppo-
sta della casa nel fronte rivolto verso il lago, dove la costruzione si
raccorda all'andamento del terreno tramite un basamento a grado-
ni in pietra locale. Al piano terra una pensilina in aggetto protegge
l'ingresso pavimentato in pietra come i gradini della scala, spazio
passante rivolto al portico retrostante, ottenuto sotto la nuova balconata di acciaio su cui si affaccia anche l'ampio soggiorno pavimentato con parquet a listoni di Douglas. Nella zona rivestita ester-
namente in pietra, di raccordo con il terreno digradante, è ricavata
una camera da letto affiancata da un bagno e da una cabina armadio passante. Posizionato tra ingresso e cucina, si sviluppa lo spazio a doppia altezza dove si sviluppa la scala che porta al primo
piano. Qui una passerella sospesa collega le stanze al terrazzo
coperto esterno. Un ampio studio anticipa l'ingresso alla grande
camera da letto padronale con bagno e zona armadi, affacciata sul
portico di testata sotto la massiccia struttura in legno della copertura.

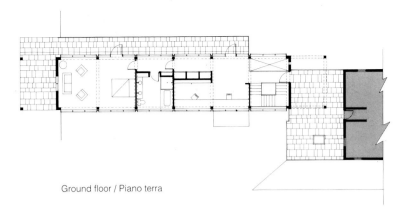

Ground floor / Piano terra

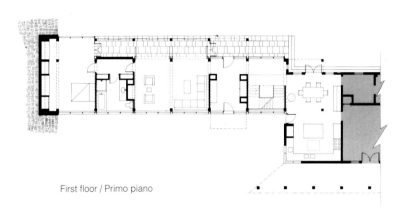

First floor / Primo piano

89

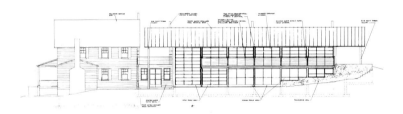

North elevation / prospetto nord

East elevation / Prospetto est

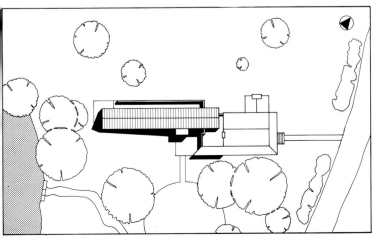

South elevation / Prospetto sud

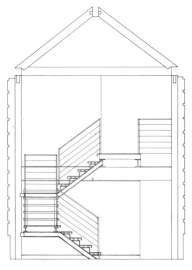

CLASSICAL AND ROMANTIC

Michael Graves Architect, Princeton, New Jersey

For his own home, Michael Graves, one of the foremost figures of American Postmodernism, chose an old warehouse built in 1926 in the vicinity of Princeton University. While the building underwent a complete overhaul, the basic L-shaped floor plan around an inner yard, originally used as a loading bay, was retained. This enclosure has been transformed into an Italian garden, with entrance pathway flanked by shrubs, alternating grass verges and gravel, terracotta vases, pergolas, and terracing, lending a distinct tone to the new house. The restoration scheme entailed creating an Italian-style villa in classical and romantic style, ensconced miraculously in this corner of the city. Graves' design is a highly creative and liberal recomposition of an existing piece of architecture, in which the building was used as a pretext for defining something quite different, erected on the existing forms, but thoroughly reworked from a compositional and formal point of view, taking a distance from the original warehouse idea. The facades have been remodeled with the addition of cornices, portals, niches, and new openings flanked by small round windows, all treated with earth-colored plaster in Tuscan tradition. Inside, the former sequence of little storerooms has undergone a total reworking by which the classically styled spaces are ordered with theatrical and functional flair. A determining factor in the new arrangement was natural lighting, which floods in through large sections of glazing, through the double-height windows, the skylights, and the oculus that crowns the foyer beyond the little forecourt. This circular foyer, a markedly classical distributive feature, is repeated on both levels of the house, creating a vertical space open to the sky by means of round openings in the first floor and the roof. From this entrance space, at garden level, on the right we have a living room with fireplace dominated by two cream-colored columns flanking the entrance to the library, concluding the vista of the bedroom toward a blind wall. The library, which occupies the former warehouse office, is a delightful double-height space; on a narrow oblong plan, the room's walls are lined with bookshelf units of pearwood planks fixed to cylindrical PVC uprights (of the kind used in plumbing) painted to resemble wood. The library looks onto the terrace outside via four glazed doors built to custom, and is roofed with a large sloping metal-framed skylight, taken from a nineteenth-century greenhouse, which admits a flood of overhead light to the "Room of Knowledge." On the left of the foyer lies the dining room, also equipped with two striking columns and a fireplace flanked by two doorways leading to the kitchen; this gives onto a white double-height atrium facing the pergola, used as a breakfast room. This second vertical space is characterized by the natural light cleverly channeled from the second-story windows and from the windows alongside the fireplace, which is finished in white oblong tiles. The second floor rotunda corresponding to the foyer below, bordered by a banister with slim ebony columns and maple handrail, provides access to the bedrooms, the marble tiled bathrooms, and a neat little study. As in the London mansion of Sir John Soane, Graves' home is also that of an art collector: each room features a carefully chosen piece of sculpture, an Etruscan or Roman vase, a nineteenth-century reproduction, an item of Biedermeier furniture, forming a fascinating collection of objets d'art.

94

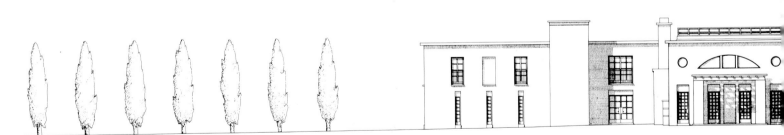

East elevation / Prospetto es

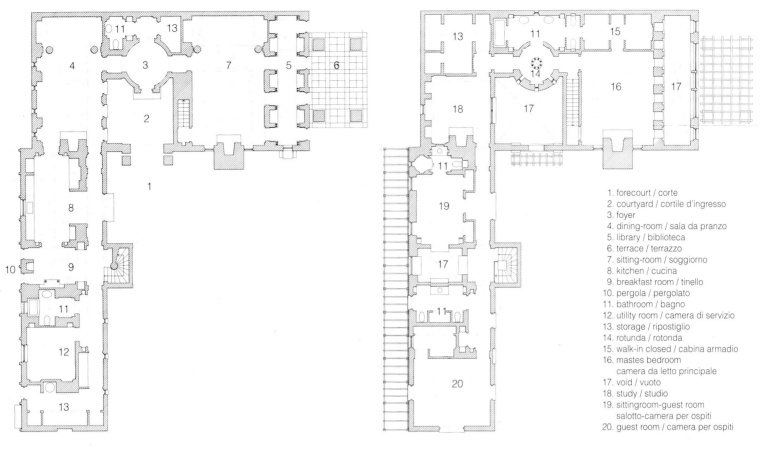

Ground floor / Piano terra

First floor / Primo piano

1. forecourt / corte
2. courtyard / cortile d'ingresso
3. foyer
4. dining-room / sala da pranzo
5. library / biblioteca
6. terrace / terrazzo
7. sitting-room / soggiorno
8. kitchen / cucina
9. breakfast room / tinello
10. pergola / pergolato
11. bathroom / bagno
12. utility room / camera di servizio
13. storage / ripostiglio
14. rotunda / rotonda
15. walk-in closed / cabina armadio
16. mastes bedroom
    camera da letto principale
17. void / vuoto
18. study / studio
19. sittingroom-guest room
    salotto-camera per ospiti
20. guest room / camera per ospiti

Per costruire la propria casa, Michael Graves, architetto americano protagonista della stagione post-moderna e oggi presente con le sue opere sulla scena internazionale, ha scelto un vecchio magazzino del 1926, costruito nei pressi della Princeton University. L'edificio è stato completamente ristrutturato anche se ha conservato la sua forma planimetrica a 'L' rivolta verso una corte usata originariamente come spazio di carico-scarico per i camion. Questo spazio libero è stato trasformato in giardino all'italiana, con viale d'ingresso a doppio filare, siepi e tappeti erbosi e alternati a zone in ghiaia, fiori in vasi di cotto, pergolati e terrazze, per incorniciare la nuova immagine della casa; un restauro d'invenzione per la creazione di una villa all'italiana dal sapore classico e romantico, calata come per magia ai margini della città. Si tratta infatti di un creativo, libero e spregiudicato intervento di ricomposizione architettonica, in cui l'edificio è stato assunto come pretesto per definirne un altro, costruito sulle forme esistenti, ma lontano per intenzioni compositive e risultato formale dalla figure della *warehouse* originaria. Le facciate sono state ridisegnate, con l'aggiunta di cornicioni, portali, nicchie e nuove studiate aperture affiancate da piccoli oblò, per essere trattate a stucco color terra secondo la tradizione toscana. Nell'interno la sequenza di piccole stanze è stata completamente stravolta dal nuovo impianto distributivo che organizza spazi dal sapore classico in un'ordinata sequenza scenografica e funzionale d'eccezione. La luce naturale risulta quale elemento compositivo determinante, catturata dalle ampie vetrate, dalle finestre degli spazi a doppia altezza, dai lucernari e dall'*oculus* che al primo piano sovrasta il *foyer* dopo il piccolo cortile d'ingresso. Il *foyer* circolare, cerniera distributiva di memoria classica, viene ripetuto su entrambi i livelli della casa, proponendosi come qualificato spazio verticale aperto verso il cielo tramite i due corrispondenti fori circolari ottenuti nella soletta del primo piano e nella copertura. Da questo spazio d'ingresso, al livello del giardino, si

sviluppa sulla destra il soggiorno con camino in cui troneggiano due forti colonne color crema, a fiancheggiare il passaggio alla biblioteca e a concludere la prospettiva della camera verso il muro cieco. La biblioteca, che occupa l'ufficio del preesistente magazzino, si propone come eccezionale spazio a doppia altezza. Ha la forma regolare di un rettangolo, stretto e allungato, in cui le pareti sono formate dal mobile libreria realizzato con tavole in legno di pero fissate a montanti cilindrici in PVC (i comuni tubi impiegati per gli impianti idraulici) verniciati con effetto finto legno. La biblioteca, affacciata verso il terrazzo esterno tramite quattro porte vetrate incastrate nel mobile su disegno, è conclusa in copertura da un grande lucernario a spioventi in ferro e vetro, originariamente impiegato in una serra ottocentesca, che illumina generosamente con luce zenitale questa inconsueta 'stanza del sapere'. Sulla sinistra del *foyer* si sviluppa la sala da pranzo, anch'essa con due forti colonne laterali e camino fiancheggiato da due passaggi verso la cucina. Questa è aperta verso un bianco atrio a doppia altezza rivolto verso il pergolato laterale e impiegato come stanza per il breakfast. Questo secondo spazio in verticale è caratterizzato dalla luce naturale catturata con sapienza dalle finestre del secondo livello e dalle vetrate che fiancheggiano il camino, rivestito con piastrelle rettangolari di ceramica bianca. Una zona servizi conclude il corpo del piano terreno. Al secondo livello, la rotonda corrispondente al *foyer* sottostante, segnata dalla ringhiera con colonnine in ebano e corrimano in legno d'acero, distribuisce la sequenza delle stanze: camere da letto, bagni in marmo e un piccolo luminoso studio appartato. Come nell'atmosfera della dimora londinese di Sir Joan Soane, la casa di Graves si caratterizza anche come casa del collezionista: in ogni stanza sono distribuiti con studiata regia le scutture classiche e i vasi etruschi e romani, molte riproduzioni di fine Ottocento, e i mobili Biedermeier che formano la ricca e curiosa collezione di questo architetto contemporaneo.

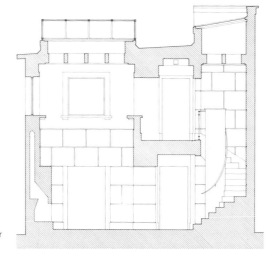

West wing / N-S section through breakfast room and stair
Ala ovest / Sezione nord-sud tinello e scala

98

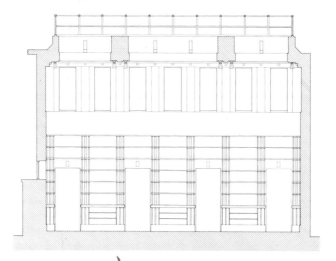

North wing / E-W section through library
Ala nord / Sezione est-ovest biblioteca

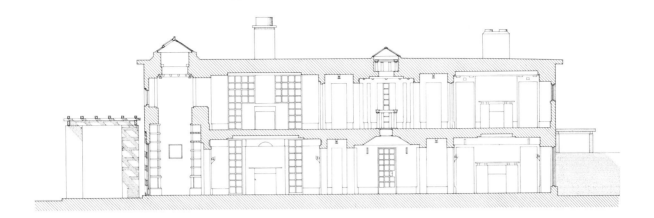

103

THE STONE BARN

Marlys Hann Architect. Catskills, NewYork

Built as a woodland refuge on the sloping hillside amid the Catskill Mountains, this compact weekend and holiday home a mere three-hour drive from Manhattan was designed by Marlys Hann for her own use, in response to her long and affectionate acquaintance with the area, an acquaintance that shows up in the layout and overall design of the new house, and in its close rapport between construction and nature. Before choosing the site itself, Marlys Hann spent a couple of summers camping in the woods, developing a feeling for the landscapes of this part of the Appalachians; eventually she came across this small grassy clearing at the crown of a hill, which afforded a magnificent view across the Pepacton Reservoir, and did not involve felling any trees at all. The shape of the house is somehow reminiscent of a hut or tent, above all for the large unitary space inside, with its mezzanine floors; but also for the tall gabled roof that demarcates the layout inside. The even cross-plan rests one of its sides on the uphill side. Two utility rooms and a bathroom have been scooped out on the downhill side, extending the housing volume without altering the strict geometry of the construction. Rooted in the ground via the underground service area, the house looks out on all sides toward the landscape, extending its interior space toward the woods by means of a broad area of *opus incertum*. This paving encircles the entire building; on the lower side is a pergola, which turns into a dining room in the summer. The close bond with nature and the mountainside is further underscored by the use of local stone (which the architect herself patiently gathered, without resorting to quarries) for the construction of all the perimeter walls, which therefore offer this stone facing both inside and out. A reinforced concrete beam supports the roof and links the walls, marking the end of the load-bearing wall and the start of the tall tympanums that continue upward in the same stone, and are punctuated by round windows that give light to the two symmetrical mezzanine floors above the bedroom and dining area; and to the spacious living room that overlooks the pergola. The roof, which is steeply gabled, is clad in flat tiles of cedarwood in the local shingle style; the roof of the bathroom, set into the slope at the back of the house, is in metal and glass. Resting directly on the slope, this glazed unit, whose shape and dimensions reflect those of the timber roof that crowns it, offers a calibrated counterpoint of materials and composition, generating a light and airy bathroom that looks heavenward. The kitchen space between the main area and the bathroom is designed as a self-sufficient, separate construction, with the cooking unit wedged between two tall sections of stone walling. An iron fireplace rises to form a curious vertical flue that underlines the symmetry of the layout and height of the roof. The high ceilings are high plastered surfaces that give a light and airy sense in contrast with the solid stone walls supporting them. At ninety degrees, forming the other axis of the cross-plan, the two mezzanine spaces of the dining space and bedroom are open onto the main living room area and toward the outside. The large windows interrupting the stone frontage help to reinforce the sense of integration between inside and out, which is particularly intriguing during the winter months, when it seems as if one is sleeping on a snow-covered field.

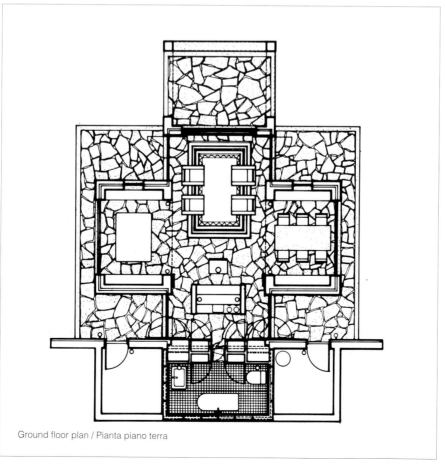

Ground floor plan / Pianta piano terra

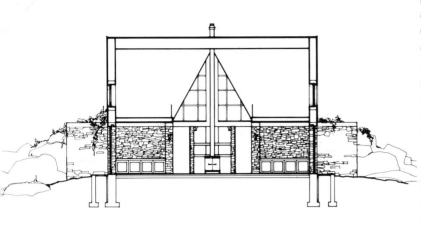

Section A-A / Sezione A-A

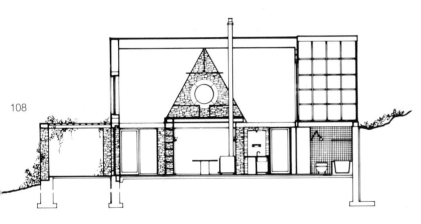

Section B-B / Sezione B-B

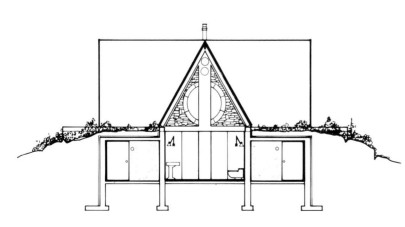

Section C-C / Sezione C-C

Costruita come rifugio nel verde, seguendo il pendio del terreno sulla vetta di una montagna di Catskills, questa piccola casa per i week-end e le vacanze a sole tre ore d'auto da Manhattan è stata progettata da Marlys Hann per sè stessa, seguendo un percorso affettivo e di conoscenza con il luogo che ha sottolineato, nel processo compositivo e nell'idea generale, lo stretto rapporto tra costruzione e natura. Prima di scegliere il lotto per costruire la propria casa-rifugio, Marlys Hann ha trascorso un paio di vacanze estive viaggiando in questi boschi con la tenda, apprezzando la natura e i paesaggi di queste montagne, sino a trovare uno spazio erboso libero, una piccola radura in mezzo agli alberi e sulla cima del pendio, da cui osservare lo splendido paesaggio della *Pepacton Reservoir* e in cui poter costruire senza tagliare alcun albero. La forma della casa ricorda in qualche modo una capanna o una grande tenda, anzitutto nello spazio unitario che ne caratterizza l'interno con soppalchi, ma anche nell' alta copertura a falda spiovente incrociata che sottolinea la soluzione distributiva. La pianta cruciforme regolare appoggia uno dei sui lati verso la montagna. Sotto il terreno in pendenza sono ricavati due utili depositi e il bagno che estendono lo spazio della casa senza alterarne la rigorosa geometria costruttiva. Radicata nel terreno tramite la zona ipogea dei servizi, la casa apre ogni suo lato verso il paesaggio, estendendo lo spazio interno verso il verde tramite un ampio spazio pavimentato in pietra a opus incertum. Tale pavimentazione circonda tutto il perimetro della costruzione; verso valle vi trova posto anche una pergola, che nelle stagioni estive si trasforma in stanza da pranzo all'aria aperta. Lo stretto legame con la natura e la montagna viene anche sottolineato dall'impiego della pietra locale (pietre raccolte con pazienza da Marlys Hann che ha scelto quelle più regolari senza fornirsi in alcuna cava) per la costruzione di tutti i muri perimetrali che offrono così lo stesso aspetto materico sia in facciata, sia nell'interno. Una trave in cemento armato, di coronamento e tenuta lega le pareti, segna la fine del muro portante e l'inizio degli alti timpani che proseguono con la stessa pietra sottostante, segnati da oblò centrali che portano luce sia ai due soppalchi simmetrici ricavati sopra camera da letto e zona pranzo, sia all'ampia zona giorno centrale affacciata sulla pergola. Il tetto, anche per la forte pendenza, è rivestito con tegole piatte in legno di cedro secondo la tecnica Shingle di costruzione locale, mentre la copertura del bagno, incassato con tre lati ciechi nel terreno retrostante, è in ferro e vetro. Appoggiato direttamente alla quota del pendio, questo volume vetrato, che segue nella sagoma e nella dimensione la copertura lignea cui si annette, si propone come calibrato contrappunto materico e compositivo che permette di caratterizzare il bagno come spazio luminoso aperto verso il cielo. Il volume cucina separa il bagno dalla zona centrale, configurandosi come costruzione interna indipendente e compiuta, con il piano di cottura incastrato tra due alti setti in pietra. Un camino in ghisa è posizionato alle spalle della cucina verso il soggiorno. Dal camino si sviluppa il suggestivo tubo verticale di esalazione, che sottolinea la simmetria dell'impianto distributivo e l'altezza della copertura. Gli alti soffitti sono intonacati e candidi, offrendo una sensazione di leggerezza rispetto ai muri in pietra su cui poggiano. Ruotati di novanta gradi per formare l'altro lato della croce, i due spazi soppalcati e più raccolti di sala da pranzo e camera da letto si fronteggiano aperti sia verso la zona centrale, sia verso i prati dell'esterno. Le grandi vetrate che interrompono le facciate in pietra contribuiscono a rafforzare il senso d'integrazione tra esterno e interno, il che risulta particolarmente suggestivo nei mesi invernali, quando sembra di poter dormire su un prato innevato.

LA GEOMETRIA COME STRUTTURA
GEOMETRY AS STRUCTURE

Steven Holl Architect. Martha's Vineyard, Massachusetts

In one of his minor novels Herman Melville recounts the lives of an Indian tribe that built a house on the remains of a whale washed up on the beach, defining a type of building based on an animal skeleton. Steven Holl has used this metaphor for the design of this house rooted in the sand dunes along the Atlantic waterfront, a natural setting of breathtaking beauty. A fundamental chapter in Holl's design output this timber construction, besides posing as a stylized skeleton of organic matter, the compositional elements and formal results of this timber construction neatly encapsulate the main poetic tenets of this contemporary American architect. A dominant feature is the use of geometry as a means of establishing order, an element of control and compositional endorsement, but also as a means of anchoring the building to the site itself, not so much in terms of the regional style as of a more subtle attitude composed of allusions, analogies, and metaphors, with undoubtedly more poetical results than would be achieved by a mere revivalist approach. In this house, in addition to the literary

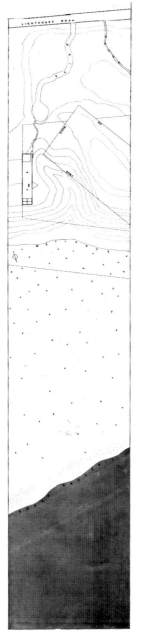

reference cited above, myriad other reminders conspire to create an interweaving pattern by means of the old technique of housebuilding involving the use of timber balloon frames, in this case left exposed to view to lend a visual gridwork to the construction as a whole. Local building laws required the house to be set back from the beach and the use of natural woods smoothed by the wind and sand, and bleached by the sun to achieve that characteristic gray tone that only long-term weathering can bring. Wood was therefore used in a total sense, as a structural element in the revival of the balloon frame, and in the traditional facade of layered shingles. The regular parallelepiped of the house itself is surrounded by verandahloggias on three sides, interrupted by specific variations that take place in a carefully studied condensation of space within the regular geometrical grid of the wooden loggia pillars (which can double up as props for local vines) that demarcate the building's perimeter. The spaces start from an ample seaward verandah overlooked by a bright living room screened from the kitchen and dining area by a large fireplace in stone and sculpted concrete; the cooker and copper ventilator hood are set directly into the back of the fireplace. This striking vertical element marking the day area is coupled with a large thick triangular window which, like a ship's prow, cleaves the perimeter of the building, thrusting out into the landscape and is inverted in the roof by the pyramid skylight. Two bedrooms are situated in the rear of the house, set back from the line of loggias, which break into irregular balustrades level with bedrooms. This feature is repeated for the sun deck of the only first-floor room, the master bedroom, which characterizes the part of the house facing away from the sea, offering a compact double-height room that neatly summarizes the overall intentions of the architect to create a brilliant interplay of interlocking geometries that embody his characteristic methodological rigor.

Melville in una novella che anticipa di qualche anno il suo libro più famoso, "Moby Dick", descrive le vicende di una tribù indiana che costruì una casa sopra i resti di una balena arenata sulla spiaggia, definendo così un tipo abitativo fondato sulle forme di uno scheletro animale. A tale metafora letteraria fa riferimento Steven Holl nel progetto di questa casa radicata sulle dune di sabbia di fronte all'Oceano Atlantico, in un paesaggio naturale di grande impatto. Parte fondamentale della produzione progettuale di Holl, questa costruzione di legno, oltre a proporsi come moderna metafora di uno scheletro organico stilizzato, sintetizza nei suoi elementi compositivi e nel risultato formale i principali punti della poetica di questo protagonista dell'architettura americana contemporanea. Anzitutto l'uso della geometria come parametro ordinatore, elemento di controllo e di garanzia compositiva, ma anche strumento di ancoraggio al sito, non tanto dal punto di vista stilistico e regionale, ma in quanto parte di un atteggiamento più sottile, fatto di rimandi, allusioni, analogie e metafore, dai risultati certamente più poetici di un semplice revival storicistico. In questa casa, oltre al richiamo letterario citato, sono presenti altre memorie che convergono verso la definizione di una vera e propria poetica dell'incastro attraverso l'uso dell'antica tecnica costruttiva in legno del *balloon frame,* in questo caso lasciato a vista e denunciato come geometria strutturale dell'intera costruzione. Dettagliate prescrizioni locali imponevano l'arretramento della casa rispetto alla spiaggia e l'impiego del legno naturale eroso dal vento e scolorito dal sole per raggiungere quella tonalità grigio pallido che solo l'uso e il tempo possono dare. Il legno è stato così impiegato in modo totale sia come elemento strutturale nella rivisitazione geometrica del *balloon frame,* sia nel rivestimento di facciata secondo la tradizione *Shingle Style* a doghe orizzontali inclinate. Il parallelepipedo regolare che caratterizza la forma della casa è circondato da portici-veranda continui su tre lati ed è movimentato da una serie di episodi distinti, uniti in una studiata sintesi volumetrico-spaziale all'interno della maglia geometrica regolare scandita dai pilastrini di legno (pensati anche come possibile sostegno dei vitigni locali) chiamati a segnarne con precisione i confini dimensionali. Gli spazi si articolano partendo da un'ampia veranda rivolta verso il mare su cui si affaccia il luminoso soggiorno separato da cucina e sala da pranzo tramite un grande camino in pietra e cemento lavorato che nella parte retrostante ospita la cappa in rame sopra i fornelli. A questo soggetto compositivo verticale che segna fortemente lo spazio della zona giorno si aggiunge la grande e fitta vetrata triangolare che, come una prua navale, spezza il perimetro regolare della costruzione per spingersi verso il paesaggio dell'intorno e si ribalta virtualmente sul tetto nel disegno del lucernario piramidale. Due stanze da letto si sviluppano verso il retro della casa, arretrate sotto i portici segnati, in corrispondenza delle camere, da una serie di balaustre lignee ad orditura irregolare. Queste si ripetono anche sulla terrazza solarium dell'unica stanza del primo piano, la camera da letto padronale che caratterizza la parte della casa rivolta verso la campagna come volume compatto a doppia altezza, episodio architettonico conclusivo di una brillante sintesi compositiva giocata su calibrati incastri e sull'uso poetico della geometria, intesa come rigore metodologico di riferimento.

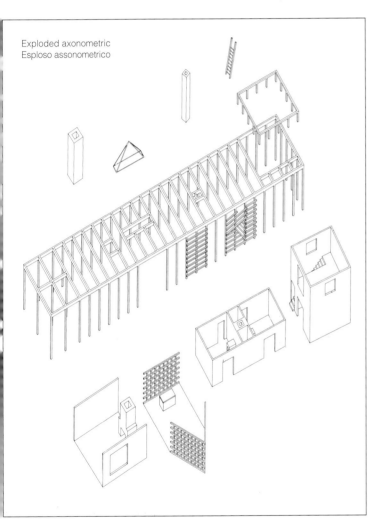

Exploded axonometric
Esploso assonometrico

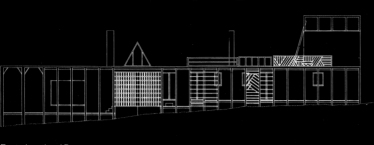

East elevation / Prospetto est

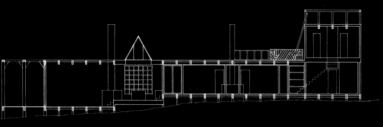

East section / Sezione est

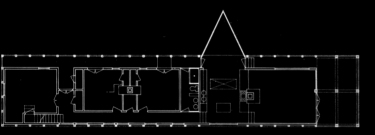

First level / Primo piano

Ground level / Piano terreno

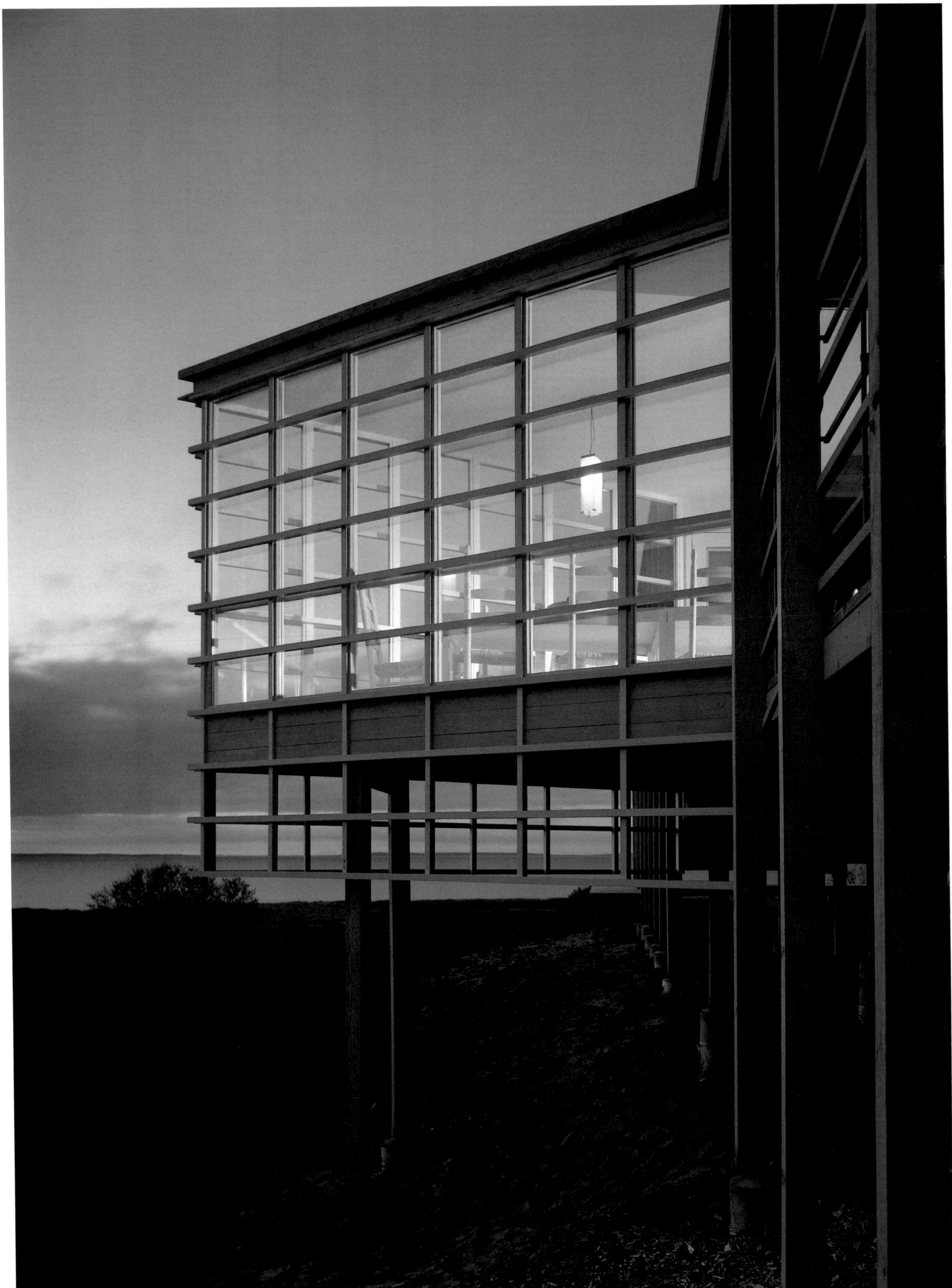

GRAFTING ONTO THE PAST

William Leddy Architect. Chester Country, Pennsylvania

124

Situated downstate in southeast Pennsylvania, in a countryside spangled with strong reminders of the agricultural communities of the early 1800s, this old stone barn built in 1820 has been converted into a three-story home. A radical restructuring project which, besides the painstaking restoration of the original structure, involved building a new extension nearby to house a painter's studio, connected to the house via a straight path of stone flags. The restoration operation shows the utmost sensitivity to the surrounding countryside (with perimeter walling in local stone, and the existing wooden fences repaired), and respect for the geometry of the original barn: a typical oblong building with thick stone walls, few windows, and simple gable roof. The old building was therefore the point of reference for a new architecture that would stand out for its choice of materials and geometry. The thick stone walls became a kind of architectural shell, a reminder of the past vernacular, conserved in the addition of a few narrow vertical windows that in no way affect the original figure. A wall in untreated metal sheeting closes one side of the ample porch toward the lawns, and two essential volumes clad in the same material – a wedge-shaped unit and a striking cylinder – were added to the end of the barn, respectively containing the new fireplace and the various exhaust ducts, and a first-floor bathroom with a small round terrace at the summit. New compositional elements in open dialogue with the existing architecture of the site, like the old wooden silos standing alongside the barn, which, together with the stable converted into garage, testify to the original agricultural functions of the farmstead. The interiors involve a new inner shell detached from the stone walls. Skillfully grafted onto the past, this new living space is a elaborate design in burnished steel with perimeter walls clad in cherrywood on the outside, and white plaster on the inside. Eschewing stylistic mixing, the design is boldly modern both in its distribution of volumes and in its attention to detail and choice of materials. The new spaces are arranged within the new perimeter walls, while the full-height space between the old and new constructions is an emblematic confrontation of past and present, from where the staircases depart for the various levels. On the ground floor, level with on the lower section of the porch, are the living room and dining area, flanked by a connecting kitchen. The contrast between new solutions and traces of the past is particularly evident in the original ceiling, with its solid beams of tree trunks. The same atmosphere continues on next first floor up, where the old beams are exposed via a cutaway in the maplewood floor opposite the entrance, which, set back from the large full-height doorway in the stone frontage, presents a new image of the house, offering a glimpse of the second wooden shell inside, with its metal canopy. In line with the central gap, which separates a little office from the guest bedroom, the space rises to double height so as to draw light from the new attic windows above. Here one obtains a view of the roofing and the suspended walkway, contained between plates of sanded glass set into a steel framework, which on the second story link up the bedrooms in the night area situated in the ample loft.

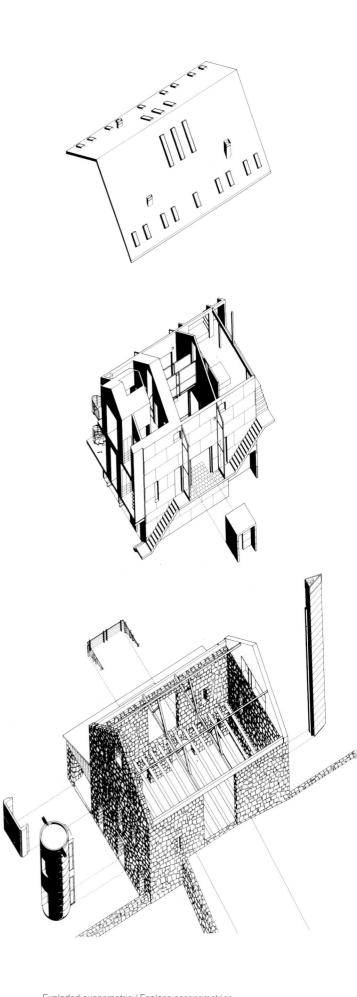

Exploded axonometric / Esploso assonometrico

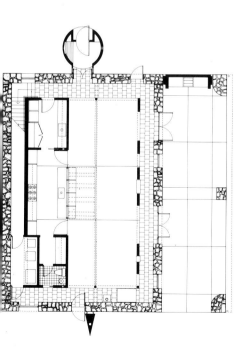
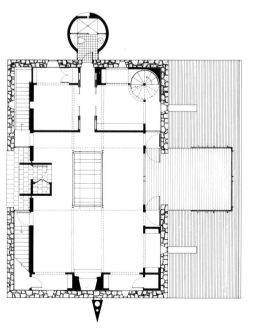
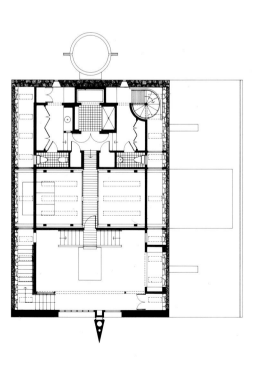

Ground floor / Piano terra

First floor / Primo piano

Second floor / Secondo piano

Nella campagna del sud est della Pennsylvania, che conserva ancora antiche tracce degli insediamenti agricoli dell'inizio del secolo scorso, è stato trasformato un vecchio granaio in pietra costruito nel 1820, ricavandone una residenza su tre livelli. Un progetto di ristrutturazione radicale che oltre al creativo e significativo recupero dell'antica struttura ha affiancato una nuova costruzione poco lontana per ospitare uno studio di pittura, collegato alla casa con un sentiero rettilineo di pietra nel prato. Il progetto di restauro ha operato con grande attenzione, nel totale rispetto sia del paesaggio limitrofo (con i muretti in pietra e gli steccati di legno esistenti restaurati) sia della geometria e del volume originale del granaio: un parallelepipedo regolare caratterizzato da spesse pareti di pietra con poche aperture e da una semplice copertura a falda. Questa antica struttura è stata assunta come volume di riferimento e di confine in cui costruire una nuova architettura in grado di emergere per materiali e figure da quella preesistente. Le spesse pareti di pietra sono così diventate una sorta di guscio architettonico, testimonianza del passato vernacolare dell'edificio, conservato nell'immagine con l'aggiunta di poche strette aperture verticali che non ne alterano la figura originaria. Una parete di lamiera grezza tampona un lato dell'ampio portico verso il prato mentre due volumi elementari rivestiti con lo stesso materiale, una slanciata lama a sezione triangolare e un forte cilindro, si sono aggiunti alle testate dell'edificio per contenere rispettivamente il nuovo camino e gli scarichi degli impianti; un bagno al primo livello e un piccolo terrazzo circolare sulla sommità. Nuovi elementi compositivi che dialogano apertamente con le preesistenze architettoniche del sito, come il vecchio silos di legno che si affianca alla casa tetimoniando - insieme alla stalla trasformata in garage - la vocazione agricola originaria del luogo. La soluzione progettuale interna ha costruito una nuova architettura staccata dalle pareti in pietra e calata all'interno del guscio di contenimento. Vero e proprio innesto nella storia, il nuovo volume abitativo si propone come raffinata composizione dalla struttura in acciaio brunito a vista con pareti perimetrali rivestite in legno di ciliegio sul lato esterno e trattate a stucco lisciato bianco nell'interno. Un progetto che, rifiutando ogni commistione stilistica, rivendica con forza la propria raffinata modernità sia a livello di studio distributivo e volumetrico, sia nella cura dei dettagli e nella scelta dei materiali. I nuovi spazi della casa sono così ricavati all'interno delle nuove pareti perimetrali, mentre lo spazio a tutt'altezza tra queste ultime e quelle antiche in pietra si propone come percorso emblematico di confronto tra passato e presente, in cui sono posizionate anche le scale di salita ai diversi livelli. Al piano terreno, ubicato alla quota inferiore del portico, sono disposti gli spazi del soggiorno e della sala da pranzo a fianco della cucina passante. Il confronto tra nuove soluzioni e tracce del passato è particolarmente evidente nelle antiche travi a tronco d'albero del soffitto originario. La stessa atmosfera permane al primo piano dove le antiche travi sono in luce nel foro centrale del pavimento di legno d'acero di fronte all'ingresso che, arretrato rispetto all''ampia apertura a tutt'altezza del fronte in pietra, denuncia la nuova immagine della casa offrendo sulla facciata la seconda nuova pelle lignea delle pareti interne in cui si innesta il portantino di lamiera. In corrispondenza del taglio centrale, che separa il soggiorno da un piccolo ufficio e dalla camera per gli ospiti, lo spazio diventa a doppia altezza per catturare la luce dai nuovi abbaini in lamiera ricavati nel tetto. Qui si offre la vista della copertura e della passerella sospesa, contenuta da lastre di vetro sabbiato posizionate in una struttura di acciaio, che al secondo piano collega le camere da letto della zona notte ricavata nell'ampio sottotetto.

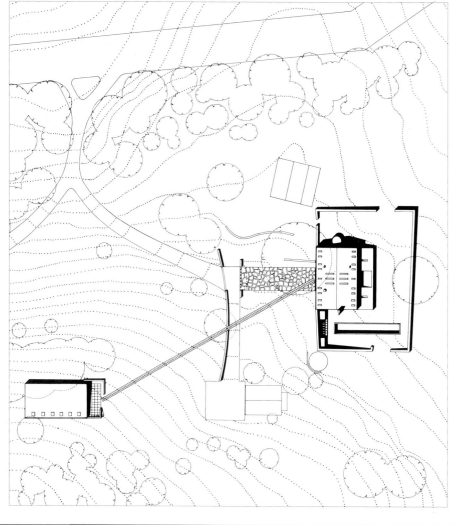

ALONE IN THE HILLS

Edward I. Mills Architect. Brighton, Michigan

Complying with the gentle slope of the Brighton countryside that dips toward the little lake, this large single-family house has been carefully designed to mesh carefully with the landscape. Composed of two separate units lying in parallel, the house proper and its wide garage for four automobiles forms a complex settlement that alternate between striking linear vessels of brickwork punctuated with small glazed openings and interrupted by smaller jutting volumes that give an engaging sense of rhythm to the over all floor plan and to the garden facade. The garden itself is structured as a series of tiers descending toward the waterfront, and lies between the two sections of the house, ranged with brick retaining walls, stone pathways, and slender steel railings. This space shielded by the two buildings but nevertheless open to the countryside is the house's most cogent feature. While the facades onto the lawns and the street behind are plain surfaces, with exposed brickwork with windows carefully placed vertically and horizontally, and a few tall windows set at the corners on the lake side, the facade on the garden side is a transparent wall in which a thin aluminum framework divides the window area up into a discreet pattern of horizontal and vertical portions. The large glazed wall facing southeast so as to catch the sun's rays in winter and thereby radically cut fuel bills, rises level with the sloping roof in steel panels, and is interrupted by lower sections that underscore the overall picture of the architecture while articulating various functions (guest suite, library, a small gym) distributed on various levels prompted by the sloping terrain. On the lawn side, the large roof composed of two interlocking elements gives a sculptural crown to the building. From the entrance a long and narrow double-height space (reminiscent of an art gallery) runs the full length of the house separating the glazed area and jutting units from the living room, kitchen, dining room, and play rooms for the kids. This effective vertical cleavage, which unites the various rooms of the house in a single space, has a curious design inside, with colored panels along a curved wall composed of plain horizontal boards (in homage to local barn architecture). This feature continues up to the first floor, where a lightweight metal landing overlooking the space below distributes the bedrooms and separate bathrooms, and spacious wardrobes. The master bedroom, situated at lake head of the house is linked to the compact but well-equipped gym and the sun deck, which is scooped out of the roof of the ground-floor study-library. The maplewood floors used liberally through the house lend connectivity to the different rooms, while offering a sense of self-sufficiency to each area.

a) foyer
b) main entry
c) gallery
d) guest bedroom
e) children's playroom
f) kitchen
g) dining
h) living
i) family
j) library
k) deck
l) terrace
m) hall
n) bedroom
o) masterbed
p) bridge
q) exercise
r) roof terrace

140

Ground floor / Piano terra

First floor / Primo piano

Costruita seguendo il dolce pendio del terreno che nella campagna di Brighton scende a raccordarsi con un piccolo lago, questa grande casa unifamilare si propone come studiata composizione architettonica inserita con attenzione nel paesaggio. Formata da due corpi separati affiancati in parallelo, la casa di abitazione e l'ampio garage per quattro vetture, il progetto si configura come insediamento complesso, che alterna a forti e lineari corpi di mattone segnati da piccole aperture superfici completamente vetrate e interrotte da volumi più piccoli aggettanti, in grado di arricchire e movimentare sia la pianta dell'abitazine, sia il disegno della facciata verso il giardino. Questo, pensato come serie di terrazze verdi digradanti verso il lago, è ricavato nello spazio compreso tra i due corpi della casa, segnato da muretti di mattone di sostegno, passaggi in pietra di collegamento e leggere ringhiere di acciaio. É qui, su questo spazio protetto e racchiuso tra i due edifici e allo stesso tempo aperto verso il paesaggio, che l'architettura della casa rivela la sua più ricca figura. Se infatti le facciate rivolte verso i prati e la strada retrostante si caratterizzano come superfici piene, rivestite in mattone faccia a vista e segnate da rare e studiate aperture pensate come sottili tagli verticali e orizzontali, finestre a nastro e poche alte vetrate posizionate nell'angolo verso il lago, il fronte rivolto verso il giardino si propone come parete trasparente in cui il sottile infisso di alluminio disegna una partitura che alterna porzioni orizzontali e verticali di diverse dimensioni in una studiata regia figurativa. La grande parete di vetro, posizionata a sud-est in modo da catturare il calore dei raggi solari riducendo notevolmente nei mesi invernali il costo dell'impianto di riscaldamento, si spinge sino

al bordo della copertura inclinata in pannelli di acciaio ed è interrotta da volumi più bassi che rafforzano l'immagine architettonica complessiva e ospitano varie funzioni (camera degli ospiti, libreria, piccola palestra) distribuite su diversi livelli, suggeriti dall'andamento digradante del terreno. Verso il prato, la grande copertura in acciaio a due diverse falde raccordate si configura come elemento plastico di coronamento. Dall'ingresso un lungo e stretto spazio a doppia altezza, sorta di riuscita luminosa galleria domestica, si sviluppa per tutta la lunghezza della casa separando vetrata e volumi aggettanti da soggiorno, cucina, sala da pranzo e stanza dei giochi per i bambini. Questo efficace taglio volumetrico verticale, che unisce in un unico ambiente le stanze della casa è attentamente studiato anche nella controfacciata interna, che alterna setti intonacati colorati a una parete in curva composta da una struttura di legno naturale a doghe orizzontali (un omaggio alle figure dei tradizionali granai della zona).
Questa si sviluppa sino al primo piano, dove una leggera balconata in metallo affacciata sullo spazio sottostante distribuisce le camere da letto corredate da bagni indipendenti e da ampie cabine armadio. La stanza da letto padronale, ubicata nella testata della casa rivolta verso il lago, è collegata alla piccola e funzionale palestra e alla terrazza solarium ricavata sulla copertura dello studio-libreria del piano terreno. I pavimenti in legno di acero di gran parte della casa sottolineano il carattere di integrazione tra le diverse stanze, che non rinunciano però a proporsi anche come colorati spazi compiuti, all'interno di una studiata composizione architettonica.

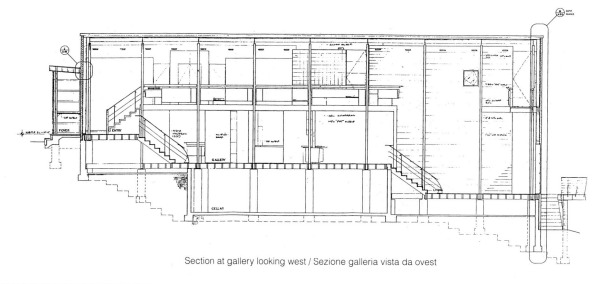

Section at gallery looking west / Sezione galleria vista da ovest

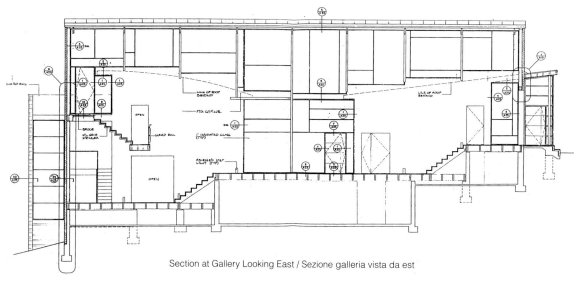

Section at Gallery Looking East / Sezione galleria vista da est

SPAZI SOSPESI
SUSPENDED SPACES

Pasanella, Klein Stolzman, Berg, Architects. Daytona Beach, Florida

This house on three levels is a clever interplay of volumes set around a swimming pool, which is conceived as a sort of extension of the nearby ocean and presents a series of airy transparent interiors that are belied by the building's exterior. Abutting the pool, the striking facade is composed of two volumes clad in a tight mosaic of pale stone fragments. The main frontage is composed of large openings and pronounced balconies cutting horizontally across the vertical plane of the facade, giving the building a sense of seaward thrust. With its Wrightian echoes, the composition of the main facade of the two blocks – the smaller of which contains stairways, services, and corridors, the larger the main rooms of the house – contrasts effectively with the large glazed surface linking the two. This feature is supported at the base by an entablature forming a kind of entrance archway presaging the triple-height lobby space inside. The house is

laid out in an H plan, in which the two side wings are hinged via full-height section dividing the garden from the swimming pool, its glass affording visual permeability between the two. The primary element of the interiors is the bridge that projects into the large unitary space of the entrance lobby, set into the central block as a sort of condensed private museum filled with tall Polynesian sculptures and Chihulli glass works. The suspended bridge, an unusual but effective domestic feature, links the two sections of the house, and its lightweight timber frame is characterized by two different bridgeheads to which the stays and slender steel balustrades of the ash walkway are attached. The former with its solid bridgehead in aluminum, scored by vertical and horizontal slits, by a perpendicular base, and by the entrance opening, contrasts with the latter, a deliberately ethereal device composed of a tall metal cornice that encloses a copper mesh, extended along the landing as a banister. The architecture of the internal bridge, complex and lightweight, rich in attention to materials, to their combination, and the detailing, is repeated at conceptual level throughout the house, giving a sophisticated character to all the rooms, well interconnected, lying within the solid perimeter. Inside this substantial architectural container the architects have devised the various living spaces as self-sufficient units linked by corridors, unusual perspectives, and by the overall cohesion of the design details. At ground-floor level the kitchen provides an architectural hinge between the entrance area and dining room. A curved maplewood wall screens the studio from the entrance, behind the aluminum base of the internal catwalk. At the first floor are two guest rooms facing onto the garden, and a large well-lit living room accessed by the suspended walkway. The living room is calculatedly lean and light: a bowed ceiling of maple hangs in the air, like a curtain, and is neatly complemented by the curving maple wall which affords an attractive backdrop and architectural surround for the fireplace and base in black granite. The Brazil cherry floor and ebony inserts form an irregular pattern that underscore the shell of this part of the house, On the third floor the two lateral units are joined via a narrow catwalk that runs alongside the bridge below, along the garden side of the central block. The smaller section contains a small study; the other a night area with two large bedrooms including the master bedroom, which gives onto a terrace overlooking the sea. The building is a clever jigsaw of complex and complete domestic signs in which the internal trajectories are expressed as elaborate suspended spaces.

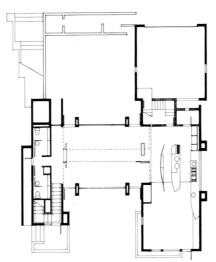

Ground floor / Piano terra

First floor / Primo piano

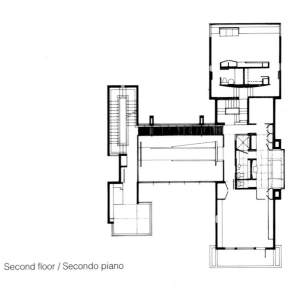

Second floor / Secondo piano

Una casa su tre livelli proposta come studiato gioco di volumi affacciato sulla piscina pensata come prolungamento dell'Oceano prospiciente, presenta nelle soluzioni degli interni un senso di leggerezza e di trasparenza che l'immagine architettonica esterna non lascia indovinare. Sulla grande piscina si innalza la forte facciata caratterizzata da due volumi con superfici rivestite da una fitta trama di tasselli di pietra chiara. Il fronte principale è segnato da grandi aperture e da forti balconi aggettanti che tagliano in orizzontale lo slancio verso l'alto dei due corpi architettonici, proiettando il volume complessivo verso il mare. Di sapore wrightiano, la composizione del fronte dei due volumi il minore adibito a ospitare scale servizi e spazi distributivi; il maggiore le stanze della casa- si confronta con la grande vetrata che li unisce. Questa è sostenuta alla base da una trabeazione pensata come sorta di arco d'ingresso che annuncia lo spazio centrale connettivo a tripla altezza. La soluzione planimetrica della casa è così a forma di una H, in cui i due corpi laterali sono uniti da un volume a tutt'altezza che divide il giardino dalla piscina, garantendone però con grandi vetrate la continuità visiva. Elemento primario degli spazi interni è il ponte che si proietta nel grande spazio unitario della zona d'ingresso, organizzata nel corpo centrale come una sorta di piccolo e luminoso museo privato, con grandi sculture polinesiane e vetri di Chihulli . Il ponte sospeso nel vuoto, inconsueto quanto efficace elemento domestico, collega i due corpi della casa e si propone come leggera struttura lignea caratterizzata dalle due diverse testate cui si agganciano i tiranti e le sottili balaustre di acciaio della passerella di frassino. Alla testata di alluminio, piena e solida, segnata da fenditure verticali e orizzontali, da una base perpendicolare e da taglio di accesso, si contrappone la seconda, pensata invece come struttura eterea composta da un'alta cornice metallica che racchiude una rete di rame, soluzione che si prolunga anche su pianerottolo come parapetto. L'architettura del ponte interno, complessa e leggera, ricca di attenzione verso l'uso dei materiali, le loro connessioni e i diversi particolari, viene ripetuta a livello concettuale di riferimento per tutta la casa, caratterizzando le stanze come sofisticati spazi abitabili, aperti e connessi l'uno all'altro all'interno dei forti muri di contenimento. Lavorando così all'interno di un involucro architettonico massiccio, i progettisti hanno disegnato i diversi spazi della casa come episodi autonomi e ben definiti uniti da percorsi, prospettive insolite e dalla stessa ricchezza nella cura dei dettagli. Al piano terreno la cucina si pone come cerniera architettonica tra zona ingresso e sala da pranzo. Una quinta curvata di legno d'acero separa la zona di lavoro dall'ingresso, alle spalle della base di alluminio del ponte interno. Al primo piano si trovano due camere da letto per gli ospiti rivolte verso il giardino e il grande luminoso soggiorno accessibile dalla passerella sospesa. Il soggiorno si caratterizza come spazio leggero: un controsoffitto bombato di legno d'acero è sospeso nell'aria come una tenda e trova il suo diretto elemento complementare nella controparete in curva (eseguita con lo stesso materiale) pensata come quinta conclusiva e cornice architettonica del camino e del basamento di granito nero. Il pavimento di ciliegio brasiliano e di listelli di ebano forma un gioco geometrico irregolare che riprende e completa il carattere ligneo dell'involucro di questo spazio della casa. Al terzo piano i due corpi laterali sono uniti da una stretta passerella che corre lateralmente al ponte sottostante, lungo il lato verso il giardino del volume centrale. Nel corpo minore è stato ricavato un piccolo studio, nell'altro è stata collocata la zona notte con due grandi stanze da letto tra cui quella padronale affacciata su una terrazza rivolta verso l'oceano. Un'architettura che nasconde al suo interno una serie di segni domestici complessi e compiuti, per caratterizzare i suoi percorsi come raffinati spazi sospesi.

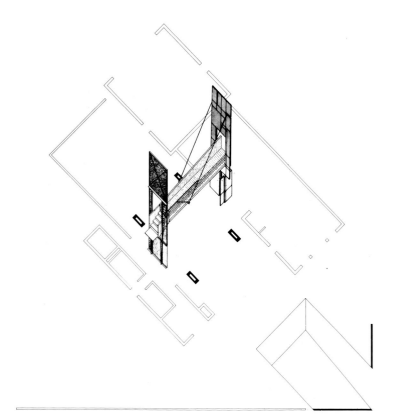

Axonometric of walkway / Assonometria passerella di collegamento

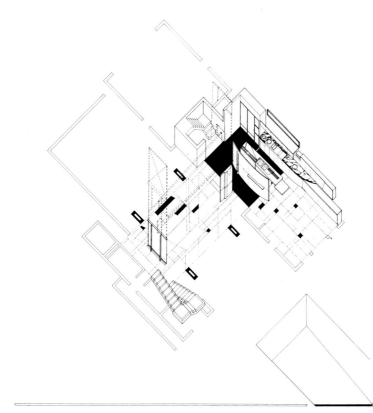

Ground floor axonometric / Assonometria piano terra

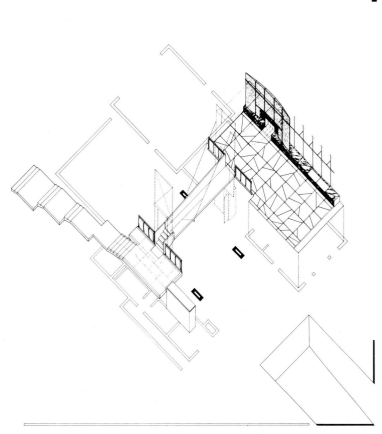

First floor axonometric / Assonometria piano primo

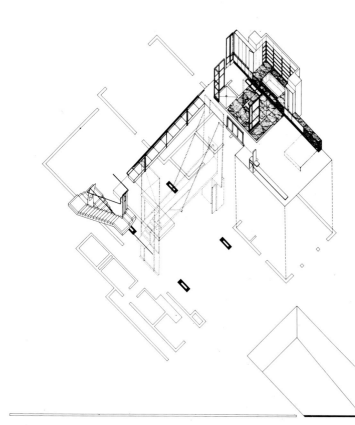

Second floor axonometric / Assonometria piano secondo

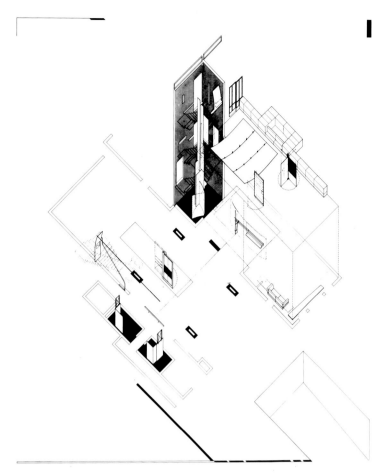

Axonometric study / Studio assonometrico

ASCOLTANDO LA TRADIZIONE
LISTENING TO TRADITION

Peter Samton Architect. Seaview, Fire Island, New York

Since the 1920s Fire Island has been one of the most assiduous summer haunts of New Yorkers. The interwar years saw the growth of several coastal resorts in the area, together with the emergence of a distinct local vernacular involving the use of certain materials, and a specific compositional grammar linked as much to the environment and climate as to stylistic and figurative elements. The unique environmental conditions tied to the coming and going of the tide, the sea spray, the lack of trees to screen the sea wind and the sun that shines unrelenting even in the winter months, has fostered a characteristic use of wood for structural purposes and for cladding, and the extensive inclusion of large sun decks for savoring the ocean sunshine, shaded areas screened from the wind, verandahs to sit and watch the sun go down. Such open areas were sometimes glazed in, as a protection against the climate and the summer mosquitoes. These summer houses were also known for their characteristic cedar weatherboarding that turned an even gray from long exposure to the elements; the uniform gray was interrupted by the white profiles of the door and window frames, and vertical white verandah posts. This

anonymous but sedate building tradition and style was Peter Samton's source of inspiration for the design of this new home in a priority site near to the water's edge. While at first sight it seems to hark back to past styles, the new house actually results from a careful study and reinvention of tradition. From a volumetric point of view the building complies with the asymmetry of many neighboring houses; these are small multistory homes composed of different interlocking volumes, with bay windows, terraces, and verandahs of varying sizes that give a sense of rhythm to the frontage and enhance the overall sense of the building. However, the house's floor plan and the definition of the facades, with their clever mixing of features (the large round window on the road side, the covered terrace, the double-height living room's semi-octagonal section facing the ocean, and the raised octagon of the garden creating a kind of open-air chamber) testify to the markedly contemporary nature of the design, a form of architecture, however, that does not break faith with local tradition or with the *genius loci*. Another aspect that denotes a departure from local typologies is the unusual arrangement of the rooms; the ground floor actually hosts the night area, with four bedrooms, two bathrooms, and laundry. The day area has instead been raised to the upper story to allow enjoyment of the view and the ocean breeze. The strong base course of the house, interrupted by a series of regular openings in white-stained wood, sustains the uneven profile of the day area with its verandahs and terrace, comprising the kitchen, dining room, and the spectacular double-height living room overlooking the ocean. One end of the tall living room and kitchen space (designed to accommodate a possible extra floor in future) looks onto a spacious porch that is also accessed via an internal stairway encased in the divider wall that also contains the larder between the kitchen and living room. The stairs lead to a further observation post that gives another view of the ocean.

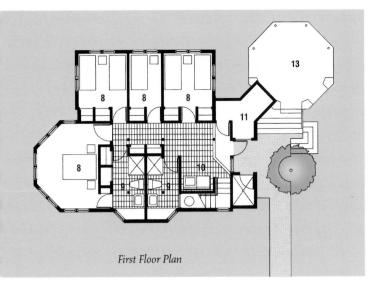

First Floor Plan

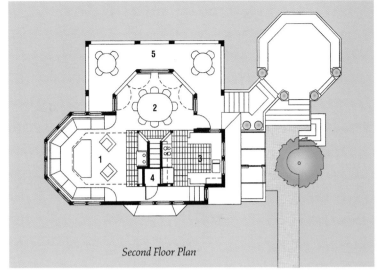

Second Floor Plan

Fire Island è stata sin dagli anni '20 uno dei luoghi di villeggiatura estiva preferiti dai cittadini di New York. Nel periodo tra le due guerre, insieme alla crescita di varie località balneari, si è via via formata un'architettura vernacolare locale caratterizzata sia da un impiego di specifici materiali, sia dall'uso di una precisa grammatica compositiva legata a contingenze ambientali e climatiche oltre che a ragioni figurative e stilistiche. La particolare situazione ambientale connessa all'andamento delle maree, all'umidità marina e all'assenza di alberature ad alto fusto in grado di schermare il vento e il forte sole che batte incessante anche nei mesi più rigidi, ha portato questa architettura locale a caratterizzarsi per l'uso del legno impiegato sia a livello strutturale, sia come rivestimento di facciata, e a creare, insieme ad ampie terrazze dove prendere il sole accarezzati dalla brezza marina, spazi per l'ombra e per la protezione dal vento come ampie verande e terrazze coperte da cui osservare i tramonti sul mare. Spazi esterni che a volte venivano chiusi, per proteggersi oltre che dalle avversità climatiche anche dalle fastidiose zanzare estive. Queste case di villeggiatura erano anche caratterizzate dalla tradizionale tecnica di rivestimento di facciata a fasce di legno di cedro orizzontali (*Shingle Style*), di quel colore grigio pallido ottenuto in modo naturale per l'esposizione al sole insistente e alla salsedine, interrotte dalle modanature bianche dei profili degli infissi e dalle ringhiere di legno a listelli verticali. A questa anonima quanto dignitosa tradizione costruttiva e stilistica ha fatto riferimento Peter Samton nel costruire la sua casa per le vacanze affacciata in prima fila sul bordo del mare. Se a una prima lettura il progetto potrebbe sembrare la ripresa stilistica di elementi e figure del passato, in realtà il procedimento compositivo si basa su una rilettura attenta e sottile di una tra-

dizione reinventata. Dal punto di vista volumetrico la costruzione riprende l'andamento asimmetrico dei migliori esempi locali; case a più livelli composte da diversi volumi uno sull'altro, con ampi o piccoli *bow-windows*, terrazze e verande, in grado di movimentare l'andamento delle facciate e di arricchire le figure complessive. Ma lo studio della pianta, la definizione dei fronti caratterizzati da forti elementi compositivi come il grande oblò-segnale emergente dalla strada, o come il terrazzo coperto e il grande spazio semiottagonale del soggiorno a doppio livello rivolti verso l'oceano e ancora la terrazza ottagonale rialzata nel giardino come sorta di camera all'aria aperta, testimoniano il carattere contemporaneo di un'architettura che vuole tuttavia dialogare con la storia e ascoltare il *genius loci*. Ulteriore differenza rispetto agli esempi storici delle tipologie locali è la diversa disposizione delle funzioni interne; al piano terreno è stata infatti ubicata la zona notte con quattro camere da letto, doppi servizi e lavanderia. La zona giorno è stata invece posizionata al primo piano per godere al meglio il panorama e la brezza marina. Il forte basamento della casa, interrotto da una serie di aperture regolari in legno tinteggiato di bianco, sostiene così l'andamento irregolare e movimentato della zona giorno con verande e terrazze, in cui sono disposti cucina, sala da pranzo e lo spettacolare luminoso soggiorno a doppia altezza rivolto verso l'oceano. L'alto spazio di soggiorno e cucina, pensato per un possibile futuro ampliamento con la sola aggiunta delle solette di legno, si affaccia nella parte conclusiva esterna su un'ampia terrazza, già raggiungibile dalla scala interna, ottenuta nell'elemento divisorio che contiene anche la dispensa tra cucina e soggiorno, per collegare la casa ad un ulteriore avamposto di osservazione proiettato verso l'orizzonte dell'oceano.

163

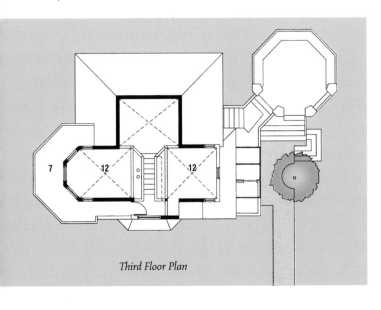

Third Floor Plan

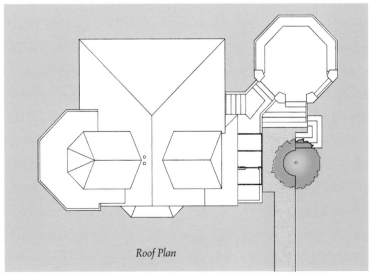

Roof Plan

Section

V O L U M I   A B I T A B I L I
LIVING VOLUMES

Schwartz/Silver Architects. Copake, New York

Built on the grassy slopes of the Copake hillside, this holiday home stands apart in a large estate with its own lake. The visual concept here was to situate the house on the gentle slope that descends toward the water facing the thick woodland covering the hill opposite. The superb rural setting with no other building in sight has prompted the architects to create a building that emerges from the natural surroundings like a colored sculpture, a landmark confidently slotted into the countryside and carefully conforming with the contours of the terrain.

Pivoting on a central hangar-type section with a large vaulted roof are several adroitly interlocking volumes. A striking feature of the complex is the difference between the facade on the road side with respect to that on the lake side, which enjoys a broader view. The general layout of the different internal spaces is reflected in the treatment of the exteriors, the road-side facade being more introvert: the plain frontage is punctuated with small square and rectangular windows in seemingly haphazard fashion. The impression of primary volumes, of precise volumetric coupling creating an almost abstract sculpture is emphasized by the varying use of color for each of the composite volumes of the building. The white plasterwork of the central section is complemented by yellow denoting the first-floor guest suite, suspended above the hillside by means of an exposed concrete ledge; similarly, gray is used for the master bedroom alongside the living room, and for the other bedrooms, which are located in the night area at ground-floor level, and visible only from the lake side. This is the more luminous and transparent prospect of the house, which plays off its somewhat closed counterpart on the road side with a series of large glazed sections of vertical panels of varying height marking the central building and rising almost to the curved roof. Arranged around and below the large transparent wall illuminating the living room are the other building sections, which on this side have large windows onto the lake. The decision to set the living and dining room, kitchen, and main bedroom on the first floor is explained by the fact that the magnificent view improves with height. The sense of space outside is reiterated by the spacious and well-lit living and dining space with its vaulted ceiling, all raised above ground level, with oak floors, stone fireplace, and timber ceiling, from which emerge elements of the metal framework bolted to the timber uprights. Grouped around this double-height space, which affords an excellent position for admiring the surrounding countryside, are the other rooms and a large patio, slotted into the roof of two of the bedrooms on the story below, which mark the extension of the gray body of the main building beneath.

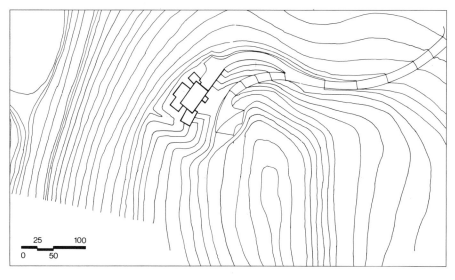

25   100

0   50

Elevation 1 / Prospetto 1

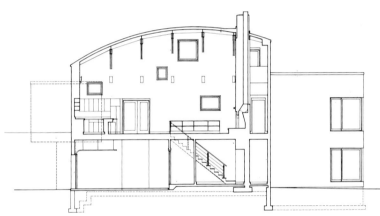

Section 1 / Sezione 1

Elevation 4 / Prospetto 4

Costruita sui prati delle colline di Copake questa casa per le vacanze si erge solitaria in una vasta tenuta con un piccolo lago privato. La scelta paesaggistica d'insieme è stata quella di collocare la casa sul leggero pendio del prato digradante verso lo specchio d'acqua con alle spalle il fitto bosco che copre l'intera collina. Il paesaggio agreste di grande bellezza e libero da altre vicine costruzioni e, ha suggerito di pensare alla casa come a un volume emergente dalla natura, sorta di colorata scultura abitabile inequivocabilmente riconoscibile, inserita con convinzione e forza compositiva nel verde della campagna seguendo l'andamento naturale del terreno. Incentrata su un volume principale ad hangar dotato di una grande copertura a volta, cui si aggregano con studiati incastri altri volumi abitabili, la casa evidenzia anzitutto un diverso trattamento dei fronti tra quello rivolto verso la strada di accesso a monte, e quello aperto a valle verso il lago e una vista più ampia. L'impostazione volumetrica generale, scandita da diversi spazi interni cui corrispondono in facciata altrettante soluzioni compositive, trova nell'affaccio verso la strada il suo carattere più introverso; le pareti si propongono infatti come superfici piene interrotte da piccole aperture quadrate e rettangolari disposte secondo un'apparente casualità. La sensazione di volumi primari, di precisi incastri volumetrici chiamati quasi a comporre una scultura astratta è sottolineata anche dall'uso del colore differenzia le diverse porzioni che compongono la casa. All'intonaco bianco che avvolge tutto il corpo centrale di riferimento si aggiungono il giallo, che segna fortemente la camera degli ospiti collocata al primo livello e sospesa

Elevation 2 / Prospetto 2

sul prato grazie a un setto di appoggio in cemento armato a vista, e grigio impiegato sia per la camera da letto padronale di fianco al soggiorno, sia per le altre camere da letto, distribuite nella zona notte del piano terreno, percepibile solo dal fronte verso il lago. É questa la facciata più luminosa e trasparente che ai pieni della soluzione verso strada risponde con la grande vetrata a pannelli verticali di diversa altezza che segna il volume centrale spingendosi quasi sino alla sommità della copertura in curva. Intorno e sotto a grande parete trasparente che illumina il soggiorno si sviluppano gli altri volumi della casa che presentano su questo lato ampie aperture rivolte verso il paesaggio lacustre. La scelta di posizionare soggiorno-zona pranzo, cucina e camere da letto principali al primo piano è stata suggerita sia dall'andamento del terreno, che dalla strada retrostante trova qui la diretta connessione di arrivo, sia dalla posizione da cui osservare nel migliore dei modi il paesaggio all'intorno. Rialzato rispetto alla quota di campagna, il grande e luminoso spazio soggiorno-pranzo, contenuto sotto la copertura a volta, si propone anche nell'interno come grande spazio unitario di riferimento con pavimento di rovere, alto camino di pietra e soffitto ligneo da cui scendono dei tiranti strutturali di metallo inchiavardati a montanti di legno. Attorno a questo spazio a doppia altezza, punto di vista privilegiato per osservare l'orizzonte, si sviluppano le altre stanze e l'ampia terrazza, ricavata sulla copertura di due camere da letto del piano terreno chiamate a definire lo zoccolo architettonico del corpo grigio di sostegno volumetrico.

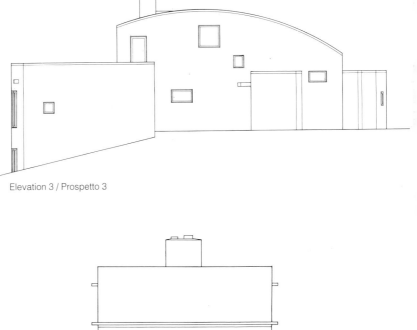

Elevation 3 / Prospetto 3

Elevation 5 / Prospetto 5

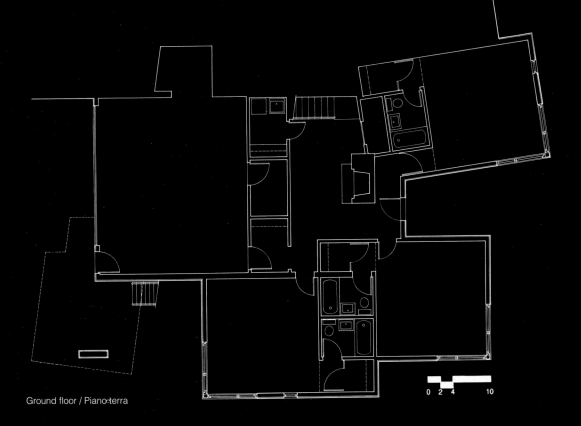

Ground floor / Piano-terra

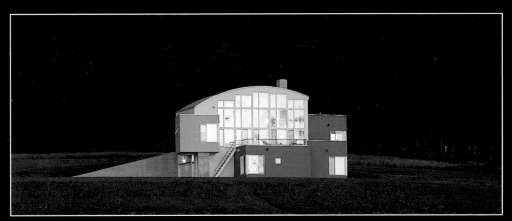

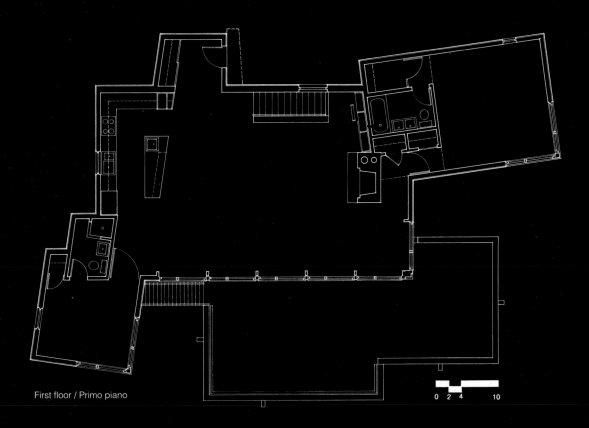

First floor / Primo piano

REINVENTING THE MODERN

Smith-Miller+Hawkinson Architects. Los Angeles, California

The complete remodeling and enlargement of a typical Californian case study built on the slopes of Beverly Hills in 1960 by Donald Plosky (pupil of Richard Neutra), evidently prompted reflection on the more successful chapters of American domestic architecture. Henry Smith-Miller and Laurie Hawkinson, commissioned to redesign the existing villa as the new residence of a film producer, had to take stock of the legacy of Neutra's style, with its magical interlocking of vertical and horizontal planes alternating with expanses of full glazing toward the obligatory swimming pool and panoramic view over the city – a formula exclusive to Los Angeles, and an indelible feature of American architectural history. Their task did not, however, result in a mere stylistic emulation or copy of the previous ideas. Instead, the two architects have completely recast the spirit of the building by reworking the original compositional scheme, replacing the strict partitioning of spaces with a free-flowing, interconnective spatial arrangement that also allows for transformation. The two primary Rationalist axes of the building (of which the entrance-pool remains) has been radically opened out, eliminating the previous delimitations of the spaces, all of which face outward. The horizontal pattern of the original construction has been maintained and even accentuated by the first-floor extension, where the new bedroom gives onto a broad patio in cedarwood, creating a set of new outwardly projecting planes. While these tend to underscore the overall horizontal feel by rethinking the roof, they also figuratively enhance the new complex living volume, which is characterized by the large glazed surfaces of the bedroom grafted onto the main block, which contains the service facilities and linkage to the new stairway. A gray plaster wall, from which emerges a horizontal metal fin fixed to a steel up right, flanks the glazed section over the stair and the triangular skylight, both elements that help define the building's new profile. The ground floor has been recomposed as a complex system comprising the hall, living room, kitchen and dining area, alternating large fully-glazed surfaces with sections of wall (finished in gray plaster with patches of exposed masonry like the outside). Cutaway sections of the roof and a rhythmical treatment of the ceilings give character to the large unitary space, where a new aluminum staircase provides a light-weight feature that helps separate the dining area from the living room. Here a second base course in stone sustains the large metal canopy over the fireplace, which is itself composed of a heavy stone lintel bearing a metal bracket for the canopy, and side walls of gray plaster. The entrance from the road alongside the garage (with its sophisticated door in aluminum and sanded Lexan) carries an eye-catching geometrical pergola, whose pattern is reiterated in the canopy over the house entrance to emphasize the longitudinal axis all the way to the swimming pool. The house's close rapport with its surroundings (garden laid out by Achva Stein, with a large swimming pool surrounded by irregular paving) is noticeable in every detail, such as the careful choice of materials, which are repeated inside and, thanks to the ample glazing overlooking the pool and city, eschews the traditional house facade and instead proposes a virtual screen projecting the living unit toward the greenery. Plans for an extension are in the pipeline; this will entail building on the side of the house, alongside the garage, following the incline, with its back to the hill, and further emphasizing the existing architectural pattern. The new project underscores the side facing the city below in its irregular L-shape, and comprises three pavilions that will contain a small screening room, a guest suite, a private office, and a painter's studio.

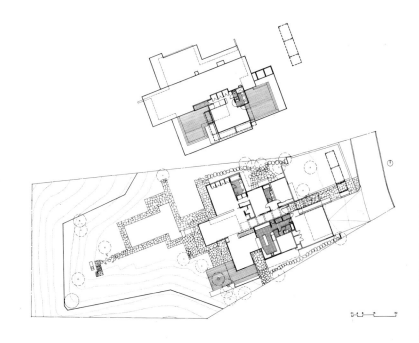

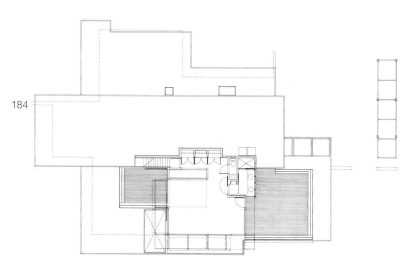

184

First floor / Primo piano

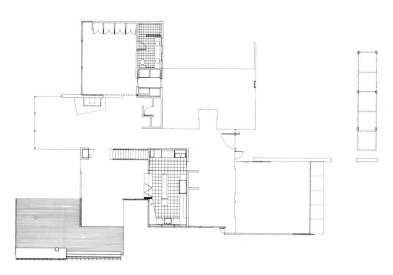

Ground floor / Piano terra

La completa ristrutturazione e l'ampliamento di una tipica "Case Study" californiana costruita sulle colline di Beverly Hills nel 1960 da Donald Plosky, allievo di Richard Neutra, è stata occasione di riflessione progettuale su una delle fortunate stagioni dell'architettura domestica americana. Henry Smith-Miller e Laurie Hawkinson, incaricati di ridisegnare la villa preesistente per ospitare la nuova residenza per un produttore cinematografico, si sono confrontanti con la ricca lezione di Richard Neutra, con quegli spazi domestici composti da magici incastri tra superfici piane verticali e orizzontali, alternate ad ampie vetrate aperte verso l'immancabile piscina e verso l'orizzonte urbano della città del cinema, che caratterizzarono una serie di fortunate esclusive architetture angelene, oggi parte della storia dell'architettura americana. Il confronto non si è però ridotto a mimesi stilistica o copia delle soluzioni del passato: è anzi una profonda reinvenzione dello spirito architettonico della costruzione preesistente. La rilettura della strategia compositiva originaria ha portato a sostituire alla rigida griglia della suddivisione spaziale l'idea dell'interconnessione e della trasformabilità; ai due assi di riferimento tardorazionalisti primari, di cui permane quello ingresso-piscina, si è preferita la disposizione più aperta e la configurazione dei limiti indefiniti degli spazi domestici, tutti rivolti con insistenza verso l'esterno. L'andamento orizzontale della costruzione originaria è stato mantenuto ed enfatizzato anzitutto nell'ampliamento del primo piano, dove la nuova camera da letto si affaccia su nuove ampie terrazze in legno di cedro, nuove superfici piane proiettate verso l'esterno: se da un lato sottolineano l'andamento orizzontale complessivo reinventando l'uso della copertura, dall'altro sostengono figurativamente il nuovo complesso volume abitabile, caratterizzato dalle ampie vetrate della camera da letto innestate sul blocco pieno in cui si organizza la zona dei servizi e l'arrivo della nuova scala. Un muro grigio intonacato, da cui si protende una lama metallica orizzontale sostenuta da un montante verticale in acciaio, si affianca al volume vetrato che copre la scala e al lucernario triangolare che definiscono il nuovo profilo della costruzione. Il piano terreno è stato ricomposto in un unico complesso

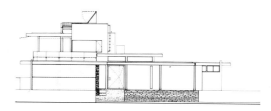

East elevation / Prospetto est

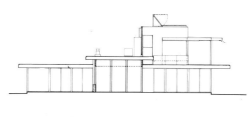

West elevation / Prospetto ovest

185

sistema che integra ingresso e soggiorno, cucina e zona pranzo, alternando le ampie vetrate a tutt'altezza con brani di muratura piena trattati a stucco grigio integrati da porzioni in pietra come all'esterno. Tagli nella copertura e studiati movimenti del soffitto valorizzano la scansione del grande spazio unitario in cui si sviluppa la nuova scala di alluminio, leggera figura compositiva che funge anche da elemento separatore tra zona pranzo e soggiorno. Qui un lungo zoccolo in pietra sostiene a livello compositivo la grande cappa metallica del camino; figura complessa di riferimento formata da una lastra orizzontale di pietra rapportata a una lama sospesa in cui si incastra la cappa metallica e dalla parete grigia trattata a stucco impiegata come fondale. L'ingresso dalla strada, di fianco al garage con raffinata serranda su disegno in alluminio e Lexan sabbiato, si caratterizza per la maglia quadrangolare del pergolato geometrico, figura che si ripete nella pensilina di accesso alla casa a sottolineare l'asse longitudinale che attraversa l'abitazione per concludersi con la piscina. Il rapporto con gli spazi esterni, con partiture di fiori e di piante grasse, progettate da Achva Stein, e con la grande vasca per nuotare incorniciata da una pavimentazione in pietra disposta a *opus incertum*, è percepibile da ogni punto della casa, grazie ad un attento impiego dei materiali, che dall'esterno vengono ripresi nell'interno e grazie al fronte vetrato, rivolto verso la piscina e verso la città, che annulla il valore di una tradizionale facciata proponendosi come elemento separatore virtuale, sipario trasparente che proietta la dimensione abitativa verso il verde.

Un nuovo progetto di ampliamento della casa è in corso d'opera; la nuova soluzione, spingendosi lateralmente alla costruzione esistente di fianco al garage, segue l'andamento del terreno collinare volgendo le spalle alla montagna e rafforza la forma architettonica planimetrica. Il nuovo progetto sottolinea l'affaccio verso la città sottostante nella forma conclusiva a 'L' irregolare dell'abitazione con tre nuovi padiglioni in cui si svilupperanno una grande sala per proiezioni, una zona per gli ospiti, un ufficio privato e uno studio di pittura.

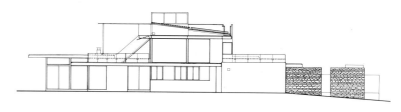

South elevation / Prospetto sud

East - West section / Sezione Est - Ovest

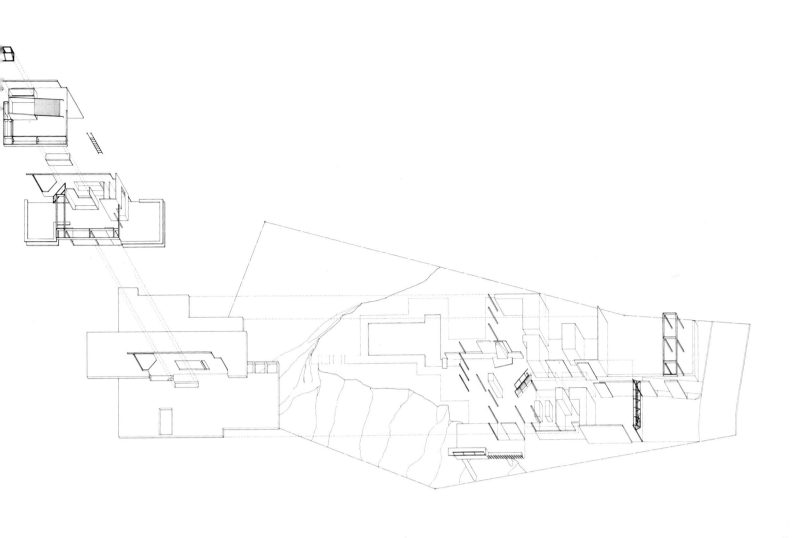

DOMESTIC COUNTERPOINT
P. Stamberg & P. Aferiat Architects. Sycamore Creek, New Jersey

In music, counterpoint is the art of interleaving melody according to precise rules of harmony, whereas in literature and cinema it tends to mean the art of playing themes off against one another. Both ideas are useful for expressing the architectural notion of counterpoint typified by this recent project of restoration and enlargement of a country house surrounded by tall trees and pools of water at Sycamore Creek, New Jersey. The two young architects Stamberg and Aferiat tackled the job of renovating and enlarging this two-hundred-year-old house with notable creative flair, eschewing the romantic idea of stylistic restoration, but without forgoing historical references or negating the inherent forms of the preexisting building, thereby successfully harmonizing the new house with its natural surroundings. The house's layout comprised a regular central parallelepiped on two orders with a gabled roof; next came a small

cottage alongside of the same shape; and a one-story garage left of the main prospect. From the outset the new scheme aimed to make use of the original pattern and architecture of buildings, and to graft new spaces and new idiom onto the existing fabric. This meant overcoming various problems of linkage, and entailed calibrated shifts and enlargements, which were achieved by resorting to architectural "counterpoint" that brilliantly reorchestrates the architecture on several registers, linked by a wholly convincing series of contrasts. The main enlargement took place at ground-floor level, which accommodates the day area; the new living room is curved and clad in pale verti-

cal strips (echoing today's farm architecture), a new multiple space that extends the house in the opposite direction to the garage, closing in a C-shape the general arrangement of the front prospect, providing a forecourt, as it were. This axis is endorsed by the footpath that leads from the little verandah abutting the living room and terminates at the swimming pool, and by the gay patchwork of wall sections (in patent homage to the Mexican architecture of Luís Barragan). The vessel of the new living room has a somewhat complex pattern: the glazed curve with its splendid view toward the water, is penetrated by the new master bedroom on the first floor above. The linkage of the two units is proclaimed in the facade in the jutting body propped on two slender white pillars and flanked by a small balcony; while inside the living room, the roof beams are interrupted by the floor of the bedroom, repeating the external motif of the two supporting pillars. An additional unit, clad in aluminum, locks into these two blocks, creating linkage with the exiting house, providing the closure of the ground story with a narrow double-height space, well-glazed and therefore allowing a flood of natural light, which offers a striking screen for the living room and another enticing view of the panorama outside. The section clad in aluminum is further characterized by a conspicuous smokestack rising above the fabric to the height of the old brick chimneys. A well-lit library, dining room, breakfast room, study, and kitchen area flank the living room, giving a new and completely reorganized pattern to the entire ground story. The first floor hosts the night area, with bedrooms overlooking the marvelous surroundings.

el mondo della musica il contrappunto è l'arte di combinare più melodie sovrapponendole secondo determinate regole; in letteratura e nel cinema viene inteso come la capacità di giocare su effetti di contrasto. Potremmo avvalerci di entrambe queste definizioni per traslare in architettura il concetto di contrappunto che ben si addice a comprendere e descrivere questo recente progetto di ampliamento e restauro di una vecchia casa di campagna circondata da alti alberi e specchi d'acqua a Sycamore Creek nel New Jersey. I due giovani architetti Stamberg e Aferiat hanno affrontato il tema di restauro e di ampliamento di questa casa di campagna costruita duecento anni fa con un atteggiamento di grande creatività che rifiuta apertamente gli atteggiamenti romantici del restauro stilistico, senza peraltro rinunciare al confronto con la storia e con le forme della casa preesistente, proiettandosi infine verso il bellissimo paesaggio all'intorno. L'impianto della casa era costituito da un parallelepipedo regolare centrale a due livelli coperto da un tetto a falda,

pedonale che parte dalla piccola veranda prospiciente il soggiorno e conclude con la piscina e il suo colorato gioco compositivo di setti murari, chiaro omaggio alle architetture messicane di Luis Barragan. Il corpo del nuovo soggiorno si sviluppa a livello volumetrico in modo complesso; nella curva vetrata che offre uno splendido panorama verso lo specchio d'acqua limitrofo alla casa, si innesta il volume della nuova camera da letto padronale ubicata al primo piano. La connessione tra i due corpi viene evidenziata fortemente sia in facciata, con il volume aggettante sostenuto da due esili pilastri bianchi e affiancato da un piccolo balcone, sia nell'interno del soggiorno abbassando e interrompendo il soffitto di travi di legno con la soletta della camera da letto e ripetendo la soluzione esterna con il doppio pilastrino di sostegno. Un ulteriore corpo architettonico, rivestito di alluminio, si aggiunge ai precedenti per creare la connessione con la casa preesistente, organizzando nella parte conclusiva del piano terreno uno stretto spazio a doppia altezza, in gra-

da un piccolo cottage laterale che ne seguiva la stessa figura e da un garage a un solo piano posto sulla sinistra del fronte principale. Il progetto si è sviluppato sin dall'inizio cercando di valorizzare e mantenere le figure originarie a livello sia planimetrico, sia architettonico e di innestarsi con nuovi spazi e nuovi linguaggi nel tessuto preesistente. Un problema quindi di connessioni, slittamenti e calibrati ampliamenti, risolti in una serie di brillanti 'contrappunti architettonici' che come in una studiata sinfonia hanno portato la partitura architettonica su piani diversi, legati però tra loro da un ricercato e convincente libero confronto. L'ampliamento più consistente si è sviluppato al piano terreno dove è stata organizzata la zona giorno della casa; il nuovo soggiorno è stato pensato come un volume in curva rivestito di bianche doghe di legno verticali (un richiamo alle moderne fattorie), nuovo articolato spazio che estende la casa verso il lato opposto al garage, chiudendo a forma di 'C' l'impianto generale del fronte principale che definisce così una sorta di aperta corte di arrivo. Tale vettorialità è sottolineata anche dal percorso

parte vetrato e fonte di luce naturale, che conclude scenograficamente la prospettiva interna del soggiorno oltre che proporsi come ulteriore apertura verso il paesaggio e il verde all'intorno. Il corpo dell'estensione rivestito in alluminio è caratterizzato anche da una vistosa canna fumaria che si spinge verso l'alto dando slancio al nuovo blocco architettonico e raggiungendo l'altezza degli antichi camini in mattone. Una luminosa libreria, la sala da pranzo, la stanza per il breakfast, lo studio e la zona cucina si affiancano al soggiorno, organizzando il piano terreno che è stato completamente ridistribuito razionalmente. Al primo piano è stata invece organizzata la zona notte, con le stanze da letto che offrono splendide viste della campagna.

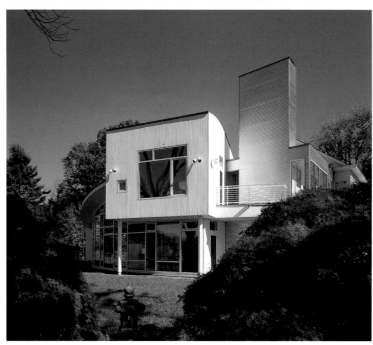

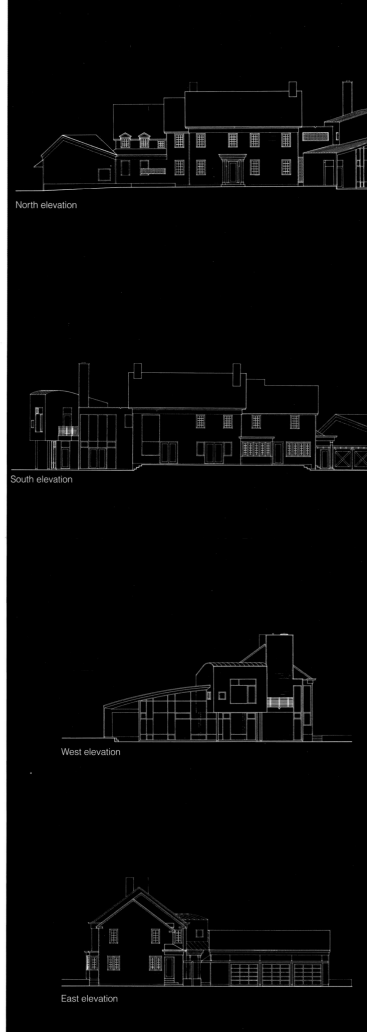

North elevation

South elevation

West elevation

East elevation

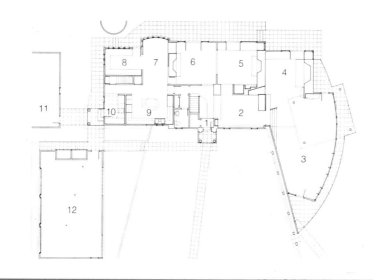

Ground floor / Piano terra

1. entry
2. reception
3. living room
4. sitting room
5. library
6. dining room
7. breakfast room
8. study
9. kitchen
10. rear entry
11. cottage
12. garage

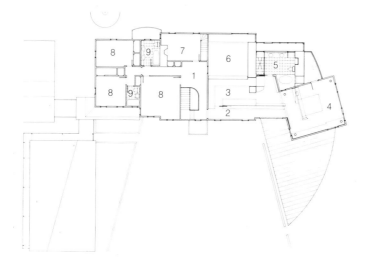

First floor / Primo piano

1. hall
2. library
3. dressing room
4. master bedroom
5. master bathroom
6. open to below
7. study
8. bedroom
9. bathroom

ARCHITECTURAL STAGE SETS

Studio A/B, H.Ariizumi, G. M. Berry Architects. North Fork, Long Island

Anchored to a completely flat wind-swept terrain spangled with low shrubs, this holiday house makes a precise statement with an unusual composition that manages to blend different building phases in a dialectical synthesis. A series of L-shaped units, like minimal linkage blocks that define both interiors and exteriors, are arranged so as to define the main perimeter of the house plan, and issue from the basic shape in the form of tall stage flats standing perpendicular to the ground, clad in corrugated aluminum sheeting. This set of striking angled sections creates an irregular shape whose floorplan endorses the asymmetry of the building's outward appearance. The facades break into each other and interlock to form an overall impression, straddling the scrubland like a dwelling object-unit of striking theatrical design carved up by the wind. The tall aluminum-clad stage flats change hue according to the time of day, separating the building units with their walls clad in cedar weatherboard, much like traditional shingling, or otherwise laid flat. These walls, which are punctuated by a series of uneven windows that enhance the facades, are counterpoised in terms of both pattern and materials by the terse geometries of the L-shaped sections, which are sometimes skewed, as are the gables, which define the complex arrangement of the building's roof. The house seems suspended over the grassland by means of a timber platform set on concrete foundations; the ground floor boasts a series of external decks that extend the interior space. Inside, the contrast between the L-shapes and the irregular walls of the connecting sections is endorsed by a different treatment of the wall surfaces: floor-to-ceiling birch paneling inside corresponds with the aluminum paneling outside; similarly, traditional smooth plaster walls correspond to the wooden sidings outside. In this manner several spaces are interlocked to form a day area at ground-floor level. A little study is tucked away alongside the entrance; the kitchen gives onto the spacious well-lit living room, whose walls alternate wooden paneling with stretches of plaster pierced with windows of different types that follow the rhythm of the roof. From the living room a wooden staircase leads up to the first floor above the study to the master bedroom; this has a small attic overlooking the terrace marked by one of the aluminum sections, which in this case doubles as a parapet. This is the highest section of the building, providing a kind of domestic tower that underscores the complex interplay of architectural features of a house that tries to create a variance of spatial experience thanks to interlocking structures that bring out the variations of the landscape.

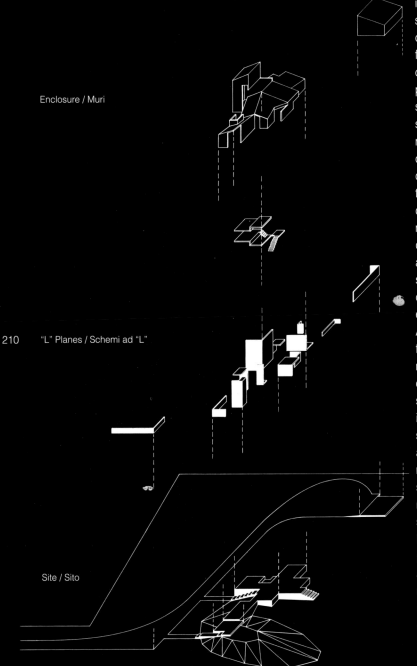

Enclosure / Muri

"L" Planes / Schemi ad "L"

Site / Sito

In un paesaggio completamente pianeggiante, battuto dal vento e caratterizzato da una bassa vegetazione, è ubicata questa casa per le vacanze sviluppata da un'idea progettuale precisa e da un percorso compositivo insolito, capace di unire differenti episodi costruttivi in una sintesi dialettica. Una serie di elementi a "L", sorta di forme minimali assunte come oggetti compositivi in grado di connettere, mantenere e catturare gli spazi interni ed esterni, sono disposti a disegnare i confini principali della pianta della casa e ad emergere dalla costruzione complessiva come alte quinte regolari e perpendicolari al suolo, rivestite con pannelli ondulati di alluminio industriale. Questi forti angoli architettonici definiscono con la loro studiata disposizione una forma irregolare che già nella soluzione distributiva denuncia la forte asimmetria dell'aspetto esterno. Le facciate si spezzano e si integrano una nell'altra definendo una costruzione da cogliere nel suo insieme, svettante nella calma del prato come un oggetto abitativo drammaticamente scenografico e scavato metaforicamente dal vento. Le alte quinte verticali dalla superficie di alluminio che cambia colore riflettendo le luci del giorno, separano copri architettonici definiti da pareti rivestite con doghe inclinate in legno di cedro, secondo la tradizionale tecnica del *Shingle Style* o posate in modo planiforme. Queste pareti, forate da una serie di aperture irregolari che arricchiscono il disegno dei fronti, si contrappongono, a livello compositivo e materico, alla minimale geometria delle quinte a "L" di riferimento anche nell'andamento a volte inclinato rispetto al suolo, e così pure le coperture a falda, che definiscono la complessa orditura del tetto. La casa, sospesa sul prato con una piattaforma lignea poggiante sulle fondazioni di cemento, presenta al piano terreno una serie di pedane esterne pensate come prolungamento dello spazio abitativo. All'interno la differenza compositiva tra le quinte "L" di riferimento fondativo e i muri irregolari dei corpi di connessione viene sottolineata da un diverso trattamento delle pareti: all'alluminio di facciata corrisponde un rivestimento con pannelli in legno di betulla portati sino al soffitto, alle doghe di legno orizzontali esterne risponde invece, dentro, un tradizionale trattamento in gesso lisciato. Diversi spazi sono così incastrati uno nell'altro per formare la zona giorno al piano terreno. Uno studio appartato si trova di fianco all'ingresso, mentre la cucina è aperta verso l'ampio e luminoso soggiorno scandito da pareti in legno alternate a campiture intonacate interrotte da aperture irregolari che seguono l'andamento del tetto. Dal soggiorno una scala in legno conduce al primo piano dove, sopra lo studio, trova posto la camera da letto padronale che sostiene un piccolo attico affacciato sul terrazzo segnato da una delle quinte di alluminio che in questo caso funge da parapetto. E' questo il volume più alto della costruzione, sorta di irregolare torre domestica di riferimento che sottolinea il complesso gioco architettonico di una casa che "cerca di creare un'oscillazione di esperienze spaziali grazie a strutture incastrate fra loro che esaltano sottili variazioni del paesaggio".

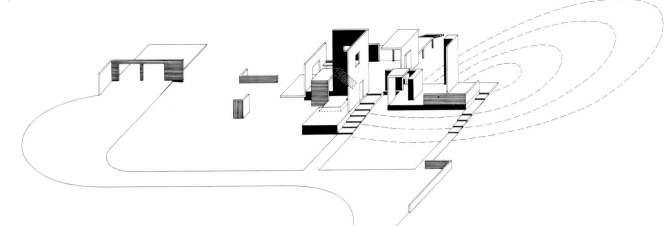

212

North elevation and sections / Prospetto nord e sezioni

East elevation / Prospetto est

West elevation and sections / Prospetto ovest e sezioni

South elevation / Prospetto sud

MICROCITY

Architect: Agrest and Gandelsonas, Architects, New York.
Design: Diana Agrest and Mario Gandelsonas
Project Architect: Claire Weisz
Engineers: Robert Silman, Associates (structural Engineer),
Interior Designer : Wal-Siskind
Site: 7.5 acres in Sagaponack, Southampton, New York

Program

Weekend and vacation retreat for an art collector. Living room, dining room, bar, sun room, library, media room, powder room, screened outdoor dining room, kitchen, pantry, breakfast area, laundry area, master bedroom and master bathroom, 3 guest bedrooms with bathrooms, housekeepers pavilion, swimming pool and pool- house.
Square footage: 8,500

Structural system

Vaulted shed: exposed glulam arches on 10"x12" solid fir columns on reinforced concrete foundation.
Bridges: exposed red cedar solid timber trusses and steel plates
Towers: steel structure on reinforced concrete foundation.
Mechanical System: airconditioning.

Exterior materials

House: red cedar clapboard, red cedar shingles, red cedar vertical and horizontal siding, stucco finish on masonry front wall.
Roofs: Vault shingles and lead coated copper on center of vault ,two towers on guest wing: red cedar shingles, glass tower and study over master bedroom: lead coated copper.,entry hall double curvature lead coated copper.
Pool- house: Stucco finish masonry wall and semicircular bar, red cedar clapboard changing cabins with red cedar shingle roofs. pink fieldstone terrace, black gunite pool.
Garage: Red cedar tongue and groove doors, beam and posts, stucco finish masonry retaining walls, grass covered mound.

Interior Materials

Entry hall: l ,limestone floors, painted steel Master Suite staircase, dry wall and mahogany steps guest wing staircase.
Living room, bar, sunroom, dining room: fir decking, maple floors, stucco finish masonry fireplace's volume
Kitchen: Stone floor, Mahogany cabinets ,granite countertops, stainless steel sinks.
Master bathroom: white (carrara) marble floor and walls ,mahogany cabinet work.
Guest bathrooms : combination color and white pattern 2"x2" AmericanOlean tiles, red cedar cabinet work.
Cost:US $ 1,500,000.-

THE WHITE COUPLE

Floors: House is oak, studio is plywood
Ceilings: house is gypsum board, studio is plywood
Glass wall: custom magonany, windows with insulated glass
Roof: standing seam steel roofing with aluminum coating
Stair: maple in house, pine studio

Inside structure

Artworks:
House prints on wall by David Diao, Robert Motherwell
Paintings on wall in studio by Catherine Mosley
Doors: custom mahogany doors by Will Parry Architectural Windows, Martha's Vineyard
Porch and terrace: bluestone
Square footage: House 1050, Studio 800
Structural system: Concrete Foundation, 2 x 6 walls and and rafters
Mechanical system: Radiant Heat
Major exterior materials: 1x6 t&g cedar walls, galvalume roof
Major interior materials: Drywall, maple floor

Furnishing and storage

Doors and hardware: Standard Doors, Baldwin Hdwe
Windows: Will Parry Architectural Windows, Martha's Vineyard
Fixtures: American Standard
Appliance and equipment: G.E. refrig. and microwave, maytag dishwasher, thermador range and oven

Owner: Catherine Mosley
Interior designer
Design Team: Andrew Bartle, Jonathan Kirschenfeld, Evans Simpson
Engineers: Ross Dalland
General Contractor: David Haust, Quadresign Chatman, N.Y.

URBAN COMPOSITION

Floor: Clear Maple, Bluestone
Ceiling: Gypsum Wall Board
Furniture room by room
Living/Dining space: Barcelona Chairs, Early 18th c. Dutch cabinet, Swedis dining set
Glass-wall: Milgard Manufacturing.
Exterior Walls: Cedar siding.
Interior Walls: gypsum wall board.
Roof: APP Modified Bitumen, galvanized steel flashing.
Interior Stair: Clear Maple treads, steel handrail.
Exterior Stair: Galvanized steel, concrete treads, stainless steel rods, steel handrail.
Inside Structure: Wood and steel frame.
Artworks: Bronze Sculptures by Else Cobb, Sid Mortenson
Windows: Milgard Manufacturing.
Doors: painted solid core flush wood.
Hardware: brushed stainless steel.
Cabinetry: custom cabinets by Vashon Custom Cabinetry.
Terrace: Bluestone pavers.
Deck: Cedar decking.
Sunscreen: Aluminum grating, stainless steel rods and turnbuckles.

MULTIPLE COTTAGE

Floors

1. Wood floors are made of Antique Heart Pine, and are milled from re-cycle old-growth material from the south-east part of North America. They are random in width and length, and have a clear finish.
2. Stone floors, fireplace hearth and mantle are made of Vermont Green Slate, material quaried in Vermont by Vermont Structural Slate Company.
Ceilings: Veneer plaster.

Furniture

1. Living Room — Sofa, upholstered chair and lamps by Pottery Barn. Area rug is a wool durey by Pottery Barn. Wicker side table and chairs by Palecek. Coffee table designed by David Coleman and built by Nial Barret.
2. Dining Room — Table and chairs of pine by Pottery Barn. Glass front shel units by Ikea. Paper shade lamps by Nagucci.
3. Kitchen — Cabinets designed by David Coleman and built by Ikea. Stainless steel, built-in appliances by Jenn-Aire.
4. Entry Hall — Coat Tree by Brauer Woodworks.
5. Master Bedroom — Bed and side tables of birch by Ikea. Dresser of birch designed by David Coleman and built by Nial Barret.
6. Children's Bedrooms — Built-in beds of painted poplar designed by David Coleman. Dressers of birch by Ikea.
7. Screened Porch — Black iron and cane chairs and black iron and glass table by Palecek. Wicker sofa and coffee table by Palecek.

Glass-walls: interior transom windows built by the general contractor, Mike Cole
Walls: Interior of veneer plaster and painted poplar in a vertical beaded-board pattern. Exterior of clear cedar board and batten in a vertical pattern.
Roof: Composition shingles in a solid red color.
Stair: Exterior stairs of cedar finished with a Cabot bleaching oil.
Inside structure: Primarily stick-framed. Some rooms use standard roof truss systems. The Screened Porch is built of cedar heavy timbers.
Artwork: Paintings by the owner — Zilla Loney.
Windows: Custom built by Marvin.
Doors: Interior clear pine two-panel by Brosco. Exterior custom built by Marvin.
Porch: See "inside structure" above.
Terrace: Stone walls, patios and stairs of New Hampshire green slate, dry-laid.

A GRID IN THE WOOD

Floor: American White Maple, varnish finish
Ceiling: Unfinished Douglas Fir
Furniture: Saarinen Table, Custom Lounge Seating, Don Mack Twig Chair, Custom Cabinetry in maple
Glass Wall: aluminum and glass curtain wall, Modu-line Series 455
Roof: Aluminum Coated Sheet Steel
Stair: Custom Fabricated Steel
Inside Structure: Three Dimensional Welded Tubular Steel Grid

ARCHITECTURAL COMPARISONS

Exterior

Walls: Field Stone, Stucco, Concrete Board, Painted Wood Siding

Roof: Standing-Seam Copper
Windows: Painted Steel
Interior
Ceiling pool: Silver Leaf Vault
Flooring: Cherry Wood, Walnut Wood and Blue Stone
Furniture: Owner's Federal Style Antiques
Sculpture End of Pool: Joy of the Waters by Harriet Frishmuth
Project Staff: Fritz Read and Jim Walker

BRIDGE HOUSE

Exterior
Siding: Cube: Concrete Board Rain Screen
Bar: Corrugated Galvalume
Pitched Roof Form: Beveled Cedar Siding
Roof: Pitched Roof Form: Standing-Seam Galvalume
Terrace: Blue Stone
Windows: Cube: Mahogany Site Fabricated
Bar: Painted Aluminum
Pitched Roof Form: Painted Wood
Structure
Cube: Douglas Fir Heavy Timber Framing
Painted Steel, Cable and Timber Inverted King Post Trusses
Base Structure of Bridge and Bar Building: Painted Steel and Cable
Interior
Flooring: Yellow Birch
Balconies and Stairs: Painted Steel, Cable Railings with Maple Handrail
Furniture: Designed by Peter L. Gluck & Partners
Project Staff: Thomas Gluck

LINEAR EXTENSION

Exterior
Wall Base: Field Stone
Windows and Doors: Mahogany
Exterior Siding: Painted Cedar
Roof: Standing-Seam Terne-Coated Stainless Steel
Railings: Painted Steel and Cable
Structure
Douglas Fir Heavy Timber Framing
Interior
Flooring: Douglas fir
Blue Stone Entry and Stair Hall
Stair: Painted Steel
Railings: Painted Steel and Cable
Project Staff: Suki Dixon

CLASSICAL AND ROMANTIC

The vestibule
The living room
Chests of Drawers: Pair of matched 19th Century Biedermeier chests. Purchased from *Rod McLennan Antiques*, London
Large Fruitwood Arm Chair: 19th Century Russian Biedermeier. Purchased from *Juan Portela*, Paris
Small Fruitwood Chair: 19th Century German Biedermeier. Purchased from *Schlapka Antiques*; Bagelsbergerstrasse 9, 8000 Munich 2, Germany; Tel: 011.49.089.280.9887
Loveseat: 19th Century Biedermeier. Purchased from *Niall Smith Antiques & Decorations*; 344 Bleeker Street, New York, New York 10014; Tel: 212.255.0660
Lounge Chairs: Designed by *Michael Graves*, manufactured by *Design America*; 105 Wooster Street; New York, New York 10012; Tel: 800.482.7777 Fax: 212.274.0722
Table: 19th Century Biedermeier purchased from *Niall Smith Antiques & Decorations*; 344 Bleeker Street; New York, New York 10014; Tel: 212.255.0660
Flower Vase, Glass with Bronze Armature: Design by *Michael Graves*, available through *Steuben Glass*, Fifth Avenue at 56th Street; New York, New York 10022; Tel: 800.424.4240 Tel: 212.752.1441 Fax:212.371.5798
Small Tripod Coffee Tables: 19th Century Grand Tour reproductions of 1st Century brasseries
Carpet: 19th Century Chainstitch Kasmir Carpet. Purchased from *Juan Portela*, Paris
Candlesticks: 18th Century Baroque purchased at *Porta Portese* (flea market) in Rome
Wall Panel: "Psyche Bathing"; panels 5-8 of the wallpaper "Psyché et Cupidon" by *Louis Lafitte*; manufactured by *Dufour*; first published by Dufour in 1816, but probably designed a year or two earlier; purchased from *Zuber* (French wallcovering company)

Lighting: Designed by *Michael Graves*, hand-made by *François Guillemin*; *Le Corbeau*; 554 Meadow Road; Princeton, New Jersey 08540; Tel: 609.799.7979 Fax: 609:799.8746; now available through *Baldinger Architectural Lighting*; 19-02 Steinway Street, Astoria, New York 11105; Tel: 718.204.5700 Fax: 718.721.4986
The living room alcove
Drop Leaf Desk: 19th Century Biedermeier, purchased from *Schlapka Antiques*; Bagelsbergerstrasse 9, 8000 Munich 2, Germany; Tel: 011.49.089.280.9887
Magnifying Glass Collection: Ivory handles with sterling silver details; collected from antique dealers and flea markets over a 30-year period
Bust: 19th Century, French, white marble bust of Ceasar Augustus as a youth; sculptor unknown
Bench: 20th Century (faux painted) bench; purchased from *Niall Smith Antiques & Decorations*; 344 Bleeker Street, New York, New York 10014; Tel. 212.255.0660
Mirror: 19th Century Biedermeier; purchased from *Schlapka Antiques*; Bagelsbergerstrasse 9, 8000 Munich 2, Germany; Tel: 011.49.089.280.9887
Painting: "Crime Pursued by Vengeance and Justice" by *Pierre-Paul Prud'hon*; 1808
The library
Carpets: Antique Bokara purchased from *Symourgh International*, New York City
Tables: 19th Century Copy of Pompeiian Brassserie; frequently collected as "Grand Tour" souvenir; purchased in Sorrento, Italy
Photo Frames: Designed by *Michael Graves*; available through *Graves Design*; 338 Nassau Street, Princeton, New Jersey 08540; Tel: 609.497.6878 Fax: 609.497.0700
Circular Etching: (MG to give info on artist and medium) Gold leaf frame designed by *Michael Graves*, hand-made by *Don Menke*; 300 Yardley-Newtown Road, Yardley, Pennsylvania 19067; Tel: 215.493.2712
The library skylight
Lord & Burnham greenhouse roof
The dining room alcove
Painting: 19th Century copy of Guido Reni's (check spelling) "Aurora"; purchased at *Leslie Hindman Auctioneers*, Chicago, IL
Table: Biedermeier, 19th Century. Purchased from *Schlapka Antiques*; Bagelsbergerstrasse 9, 8000 Munich 2, Germany; Tel: 011.49.089.280.9887
Chairs: Biedermeier, 19th Century. Purchased from *Schlapka Antiques*; Bagelsbergerstrasse 9, 8000 Munich 2, Germany; Tel: 011.49.089.280.9887
Fruit Bowl, Glass with Bronze Armature: Designed by *Michael Graves*; available through *Steuben Glass*, Fifth Avenue at 56th Street; New York, New York 10022; Tel: 800.424.4240 Tel: 212.752.1441 Fax:212.371.5798
Vessel on side table: Gold-plated brass; early 20th Century; *Joseph Hoffman*
Cup Collection: Early 19th Century Biedermeier and 18th Century black basalt Wedgewood
The dining room
Table: Ebonized Federal-period (American) table; purchased in Maine
Chairs: 19th Century Biedermeier - two were purchased from *Niall Smith Antiques & Decorations*; 344 Bleeker Street; New York, New York 10014; Tel: 212.255.0660; two were purchased from *Schlapka Antiques*; Bagelsbergerstrasse 9, 8000 Munich 2, Germany; Tel: 011.49.089.280.9887; and two were purchased in Texas
Carpet: Designed by *Michael Graves*; manufactured by *Vorwerk & Co.*; Kuhlmanstrasse II, 3250 Hameln, Germany; Tel: 011.49.5151.103.332 Fax: 011.49.5151.103.333
Candelabras: 19th Century copy of first Century Roman bronze. Purchased from *Linda Horn Antiques*, New York City
Fruit Bowl, Glass with Bronze Armature: Designed by *Michael Graves*; available through *Steuben Glass*; Fifth Avenue at 56th Street, New York, New York 10022; Tel: 800.424.4240 Tel: 212.752.1441 Fax:212.371.5798
Stove on mantel: 19th Century bronze copy of a Pompeiian stove; purchased at auction at Christie's New York
Bronze Table Bases: Tripods; 19th Century copies of Pompeiian Brassserie; frequently collected as "Grand Tour" souvenir; purchased in Sorrento, Italy
Inkwells: Miniature 19th Century "Grand Tour" Temple of Vesta souvenir inkwells; purchased over several years in various European locations
All other bronze pieces are 19th Century Grand Tour objects
Lighting: Designed by *Michael Graves*; hand-made by *François Guillemin*; *Le Corbeau*; 554 Meadow Road, Princeton, New Jersey 08540; Tel. 609.799.7979 Fax: 609:799.8746; now available through *Baldinger Architectural Lighting*; 19-02 Steinway Street; Astoria, New York 11105; Tel: 718.204.5700 Fax: 718.721.498
The kitchen
Flooring: Stained concrete custom finished by *Arcturus Painting*; P.O. Box 544; Rocky Hill, New Jersey 08553; Tel: 609.921.9474
Lighting: *New York Gas Lighting Co.*; 145 Bowery, New York, New York 10002; Tel: 212.226.2840 and *Grand Brass Lamp Parts*; 221 Grand Street, New York, New York 10013; Tel: 212.226.2567 or 68
Table: Local flea market purchase
Counter Top: Pendelikon Marble by *Petrafina*; Architects and Designers Building, 964 Third Avenue, 5th Floor, New York, New York 10155; Tel: 212.308.6400 Fax: 212.308.6424

The solarium

Table: Designed by *Michael Graves*; custom-made by *Don Menke*; 300 Yardley-Newtown Road, Yardley, Pennsylvania 19067; Tel:215.493.2712

Chairs: Available at *Newel Art Galleries*; 425 East 53rd Street; New York, New York 10022; Tel: 212.758.1970

Carpet: Designed by *Michael Graves*, fabricated by *Couristan*; 20921 Sunnyacres Road; Gaithersburg, Maryland 20882; Tel: 800.223.6186 Ext. 850 Tel: 301.258.8468 Fax: 301.977.1908

Vessel Collection: Etruscan, Greek and Roman pottery and glass - 4th Century B.C. through 2nd Century A.D.; purchased from various dealers in Europe and the U.S. over a number of years

The staircase

Bust at top of staircase: Antique original of Homer; purchased from *Rodd McLennan Antiques*, London

Landing overlooking the solarium

Chair: "Thebes" Chair manufactured by Liberty of London at the turn of the century; purchased from a London Antiques Dealer

The corridor

Chest: 19th Century Biedermeier. Purchased from *Rod McLennan Antiques*, London

Bust: 19th Century bronze bust of Ceasar Augustus

Painting: 20th Century landscape by Edward Schmidt

Hall Print: 19th Century hand-painted Pompeiian wall

Niche Vessel: Miniature "Grand Tour" tripod souvenir in paired niches

Model: Architectural model of a pyramidal roof built by 19th Century architectural students at the Beaux-Arts as a class exercise; purchased in Brussels

Landscapes: 20th Century French; purchased on the Pontneuf in 1990 from a drugged-out female artist for $20 each

The south-west guest bedroom

Lounge Chair: Designed by *Michael Graves*; available through *Design America*; 105 Wooster Street; New York, New York 10012; Tel: 800.482.7777 Fax: 212.274.0722

Settee: 19th Century Biedermeier; purchased in Munich

Stool: 19th Century painted ebony (origin unknown)

Plaster Circular reliefs: "Night and Day" by Thorbaldson; purchased at *Thorbaldson Museum* in Copenhagen

Bedroom Carpet: Sisal rug; *Stark Carpet Corporation*; 8687 Melrose Avenue, Suite 629, Los Angeles, California 90069; Tel: 213.657.8275

The sitting room

Two chairs: One is 19th Century Biedermeier; the other is a 20th Century Biedermeier copy

Small Stool: "Thebes" stool made by Liberty of London during the Egyptian Revival period; English; early 20th Century

Fruitwood Table: 19th Century Biedermeier

Small drawing: 18th Century Belgian drawing of a cow's head

Loveseat: Local purchase

Carpet: 19th Century Killim

The study

Stool: 19th Century Biedermeier piano stool. Purchased from *Schlapka Antiques*; Bagelsbergerstrasse 9, 8000 Munich 2, Germany; Tel: 011.49.089.280.9887

Desk: 19th Century Biedermeier, purchased from *Sotheby's*, New York City

Lamp: 20th Century copy of 1920s lamp; manufactured by *Europa*; Tel: 1.800.BAU.HAUS

Boxes: Various Biedermeier humidors purchased over a period of time from various antique dealers

Table: Regency Bed Stand; purchased from *Miller Topia Antiques*; Princeton, New Jersey

Carpet: Designed by *Michael Graves*; manufactured and distributed by *Vorwerk & Co.*; Kuhlmanstrasse II, 3250 Hameln; Germany; Tel: 011.49.5151.103.332 Fax: 011.49.5151.103.333

Lounge Chair: Designed by *Le Corbusier*; available at *Cassina USA*; Tel: 516.549.2745

Clock: Antique Biedermeier Clock purchased at Munich Antiques Fair

Vessel Collection: Etruscan, Greek and Roman pottery and glass - 4th Century B.C. through 2nd Century A.D.; purchased from various dealers in Europe and the U.S. over a number of years

Paired Column Mahogany Frame: 18th Century; purchased in Sorrento, Italy

The master bathroom

Flooring: Rojo Alicante and Gris Di Quesa marble

Basins: Late 19th Century porcelain basins. Purchased from *Howard Kaplan*, New York City

Basin Fittings: Purchased from *Czech & Speake*, London

Bench: 19th Century American; purchased from *Niall Smith Antiques & Decorations*; 344 Bleeker Street, New York, New York 10014; Tel: 212.255.0660

Lighting: Designed by *Michael Graves*, hand-made by *François Guillemin*; *Le Corbeau*; 554 Meadow Road, Princeton, New Jersey 08540; Tel. 609.799.7979 Fax: 609.799.8746; now available through *Baldinger Architectural Lighting*; 19-02 Steinway Street; Astoria, New York 11105; Tel: 718.204.5700 Fax: 718.721.4986

The master bedroom

Chair: 19th Century Biedermeier

Pedestal under circular window: 19th Century American neo-classical pedestal purchased at the *First Regiment Armory Antiques Show*, New York City

Figure: 19th Century standing male figure; copy from the antique; purchased from *Rodd McLennan Antiques*, London

Two small paintings: Italian landscapes; one is 20th Century by *Edward Schmidt*; the other is 19th Century by an unknown Venetian painter; purchased in Venice, Italy

Figure: 19th Century bronze "Grand Tour" object; purchased from *Niall Smith Antiques & Decorations*; 344 Bleeker Street, New York, New York 10014; Tel 212.255.0660

Painting: "The Virgin Mary," 19th Century Academic American; artist unknown

Table: Tripod; Mahogany with black marble top; 19th Century French Empire purchased from *Rod McLennan Antiques*, London

Ebony Shell-back Chair: 19th Century Biedermeier; purchased from *Schlapka Antiques*; Bagelsbergerstrasse 9, 8000 Munich 2, Germany; Tel: 011.49.089.280.9887

Klismos Chair: Early 20th Century American

Bust: 19th Century casting of Head of a Youth from the antique; purchased from the Pearson Museum in Amsterdam

Bust: 19th Century copy of a Roman warrior bust; sculptor and dealer unknown; the bust was featured in the film *Father of the Bride*, starring Steve Martin

Bed Coverings: antique silks; Color: Saffron

Pillow fabrics: *Rodolph Textiles, Inc./Jim Thompson Thai Silk Collection*;; Tel 707.935.0316 and *Manuel Canovas/Silk Shangrilla*, Tel: 212.486.9230

The garden

Oil Jars: Terracotta oil jars, Mediterranean; circa 1880; purchased from *The Garden Antiquary*; 724 Fifth Avenue, New York, New York 10019; Tel 212.757.3008

Table: Local flea-market find purchase

Chairs: Honey Square Bistro Chairs; purchased from *Palacek*; P.O. Box 225 Station A,Richmond, CA 94808-0225; Tel. 510.236.7730

Copy of Praxiteles' "Aphrodite." Greek, third Century. Purchased from the *British Museum Collection*

THE STONE BARN

Floor: Random broken Blestone

Ceiling: Painted drywall

Furniture: Living room - Adirondack Chairs, handmade wood

Dining room - Blestone table top set on concrete chimney blocks; 'sardegna' steel chairs.

Glass walls, windows and doors: insulating glass with bronze duranodic aluminium frames

Walls: fieldstone; white ceramic mosaic unglazed tiles in the bahroom

Roof: cedar shingle

Stairs: rolling library laddres

Artwork: antique quilt on the bed terrace: stone pavers saet in sand, with cedar wood trellis

GEOMETRY AS STRUCTURE

Program: Residence
Client: Steven Berkowitz, Janet Odgis
Project Team: Peter Lynch, Ralph Nelson, Peter Shinoda, Stephen Cassell
Net floor area: 2800 sq. ft.

Concept

The site is a hill overlooking the Atlantic Ocean as it meets Vineyard Sound. A strict planning code determines that the house must be set back from the marshland as well as from a no-build zone on a hill and that it should have a one story elevation when viewed from the beach. Also the code stipulates that the house must be built in a natural weathered grey color wood.

In the locally inspired novel Moby Dick, Melville describes an Indian tribe, which made a unique type of dwelling on the island. Finding a beached whale skeleton, they would pull it up to dry land and stretch skins or bark over it, transforming it into a house.

This house is like an inside-out balloon frame structure. The wooden "bones" of the frame carry an encircling veranda, which affords several ocean views. Along this porch, wood members could receive the natural vines of the island. The ground vine tendrils transform the straight linear mode of the architecture.

The plan is a simple set of rooms set perpendicular to the view within the setback lines of the site. Beginning with a mud and recreation room off the entry there are two bedrooms, a kitchen and a dining room in a protective bay. The living room drops down according to the site. The master bedroom on the second level has a special view to the ocean across an exercise and sun deck n top of the main house.

he wood frame with 6" x 6" vertical members is treated and exposed to weather. The 2" x 2" wood members of the guard railings as well as the 3/4" x 8" board siding is weathered wood. Windows are insulated glass in painted wood frames. The fireplace is of locally gathered stones set in concrete.

GRAFTING ONTO THE PAST

Floor finish
Floor 1: Waxed concrete, Pennsylvania flagstone
Floor 2: White maple with clear finish
Floor 3: Carpet, ceramic tile
Ceiling
Floor 1 e 2: Painted Gypsum board
Floor 3: Maple plywood with clear finish
Furniture/Art
Living room
Coffee and end table: custom design by William Leddy
Lounge chairs: custom design by William Leddy
Paintings: Kathleen Martin
Twig sculpture: Kathleen Edwards
Family/dining room
Steel chair: custom design by Richard Stacy
Dining Table and chairs: by owner
Paintings: Kathleen Martin
Kitchen cabinets: Cherry plywood with clear finish, perforated stainless steel panels, Absolute Black granite counters
Glass wall: Steel framed windows, insulated glass
Walls: Exterior of "inner box": cherry plywood with clear finish
Interior of "inner box": Painted gypsum board
Roof: Cedar shingles
Stair
Main stair: White maple with clear finish
Office stair: Clear finished steel spiral stair
Structure
Exposed: Steel colums and beams with clear finish, original hand-hewn oak timbers at second floor and roof
Concealed: Conventional wood frame floors and walls
Windows: Steel frame with insulating glass
Doors: Steel frame with insulating glass
Porch: Concrete floor under existing roof structure
Roof terrace: New terrace in existing roof structure, cedar deck floor.

ALONE IN THE HILLS

Structure type: Masonry and steel
Exterior materials
Glazed brick: "GlenGery" (1166 Spring St., Wyomissing, PA 19610)
Roof: Standing-seam steel ("Dura Seam Metal Roofing," Innovative Metals 4529 Elmdale Dr., Tucker, GA)
Interior materials
Insulation: 4" X 6" batt insulation (Owens Corning Fiberglass Corp., Fiberglass Tower, Toledo, OH 43659
Windows: Desco Aluminum Windows (716 Third St. / Southeast, Desmet, SD 57231)
Glass doors: "Kawneer" (P.O. Box 629, 500 East 12 St., Bloomsberg, PA 17815)
Floors: 6" strip maple
Kitchen cabinets: Maple, custom-made
Paint: "Benjamin Moore" (1630 S. Second St., St. Louis, MO 63104)
Lighting: "Halo" (400 Busse Rd., St. Elk Grove Village, IL 60007)
Hardware: "Corbin Russwin" (225 Episcopal Rd., P.O. Box 4004, Berlin, CT 06037)
Description of furniture and artwork
Living room
Fireplace: Brick, custom-made
Lounge chair and ottoman: Designed by Charles and Ray Eames (Herman Miller for the Home)
Coffee table: Designed by Isamu Noguchi
Screen: Designed by Charles and Ray Eames
Platform bench: Designed by George Nelson
Molded plywood chairs: Designed by Charles and Ray Eames
Sofa: By Christian Liaigre Pour Holly Hunt, HXVIII
Dining room
Glass table: Designed by Brian Killian
Chairs: Toledo collection-Knoll
Side table: By Charles Phipps
Telescopic table: By Tennant & Associates

Library
Chaise: Designed by Charles and Ray Eames
Bedroom
Linens: Calvin Klein Home (654 Madison Ave., NYC 10023)
Bed and wall cabinets: Maple, custom-made
Sofa: Eames sofa compact by Charles and Ray Eames
Throw: Calvin Klein Home

SUSPENDED SPACES

Owner: Chapman J. Root II
Architect: Pasanella Klein Stolzman Berg Architects, PC, New York
Design Team: Wayne Berg, FAIA (Design Principal), Albert Ho, AIA (Project Architect)
Consultants: Jerry Kugler Associates (Lighting Design), Tse-Yun Chu Studio (Materials and Finishes),
Fu-Teng Cheng (Kitchen Design)
Craftsmen: Eric Bauer, Fayston Iron and Steel (Custom Metalwork), Jeff Vaida, JFV Design (Millwork)
General Contractor: Owner, with Foley & Associates, Construction Co., Inc.
Commissioned: 1990
Completed: 1995
Square Footage: 6500 sf
Location: Ormond Beach, Florida
Materials and technical solutions
Major Exterior materials: Fluted concrete block, glass [exterior architect: William Morgan, FAIA]
Major Interior Materials: Floor: Shellstone and grassy green slate (refectory floor), Teak with ebony insets (library floor), Idaho quartzite (bathroom floors), shellstone and grassy green slate (refectory floor), maple (kitchen floor)
Walls: Aluminum (east bridge panel), Copper mesh with steel frame (west bridge panel), Flat-cut maple with checkerboard pattern veneer (kitchen screen partition), Carrara glass with brass reveal (bathroom/shower walls), Idaho quartzite (bathroom walls), Milk white onyx (third floor translucent corner partition)
Bridge: copper, maple, steel
Ceiling: Quarter-san ash (library canopy), elsewhere skim coated plaster
Design Approach
The project is an intervention into the interior of an existing house situated on the edge of the Atlantic Ocean. The house, constructed of fluted concrete block, is seen as a massive monolith. The intervention, while maintaining the house's volumetric organization, contrasts with the shell's massiveness through the careful insertions of planar elements, e.g. screens, pivot panels, linear banquettes, etc. These insertions reinforce inherent spatial sequences and accommodate the client's programmatic requirements. In many ways, the design pays homage to such modern masters as Chareau, Scarpa, Breuer and Gray through the spirit of the details and the assemblage of materials.
Indeed the details celebrate the intricate joinery of disparate materials.

The main organizer of the house is a triple volume refectory. This space, gfully glazed on the east, is a spatial extension of the ocean into the house.
It further acts as a connector between three open floors and the to the north and the foyer to the south. The main intervention consists of two three story aluminum and copper mesh screens supporting a cantilevered wood bridge spanning the refectory. The assemby brackets the edges of the refectory and mediates between the refectory with its grand scale and the more intimate single volume open floors which overlook the refectory.

Similarly, the maple screen in the first floor kitchen, the maple burl fireplace screen in the second floor library, and the translucent aluminum screen in the third floor master bedroom are proportioned to the scale of their respective spaces. The also form a counterpoint to the aluminum and copper mesh screens. Thus, an active dialogue of materials, details, and scales resonates throughout the house.
Furniture and artwork
Furniture room by room:
Kitchen - custom PKSB kitchen island/counter base in cast concrete kitchen with integral metal and colored powders and colored glass insets, kitchen cabinetry, stainless steel commercial-type range hood (Custom designed by architect)
Dining Room — dining table with marble top (Florence Knoll), dining chairs (Warren Platner)
(Ready-made furniture selected by Steven Harris, Architect, Florida)
Library - Steel library exhibit shelves, fireplace in maple burl with hand-rubbed finish, Black granite library ledge/banquette (Custom designed by architect); love seat and sofa (Jean Michel Frank, through Palazzetti), day bed (Mies van der Rohe, through Palazzetti), coffee table (Kessler, through Palazzetti), lamp (Kevin Waltz)
Refectory - Steel display pedestals (Custom designed by architect)
Artworks: Dale Chihuli (glass pieces in refectory, glass vase in living room),

Catherine Rahn (crystal sculpture in stairway, bathroom wall light fixture, and glass medicine cabinet), owner's collection of Asian and Pacific Islands artifacts (various pieces in library)
Fixtures: Kroin (bathroom and kitchen faucets, bathroom towel bars), Speakman (shower)

LISTENING TO TRADITION

Floor: Vermont Green slate in kitchen, baths, halls. Fir flooring in living room, dining, bedrooms and stairs
Ceiling: Fir wainscoting
Furniture: Mostly Built-in. Beds and Dining Room table designed by Peter Samton
Glass-wall: Marvin Windows
Roof: Asphalt shingles atop 1ΩïStyrofoam
Stairs and Inside Structure: 6 x 6 Fir posts and 3" x 10" beams with 2" x 6" tongue and groove decking - all fir.
Exterior : all cedar shingles with painted Marvin Windows

LIVING VOLUMES

Architectural Firm: Schwartz/Silver Architects, Inc.Boston, Massachusetts
Project Team: Warren R. Schwartz, Robert Silver, Timothy Downing, Elise Gispan,
Leo Chow, Jim McQueen
Contractor: David Haust, Quadresign
Engineer: Charles Chaloff (Structural)
Square footage: 3,600 square feet
Materials
Type Manufacturer
Structural System: 2x6 Woodframe
Exterior Cladding: Exterior Insulating Finish System Parex
Roofs: Rubber Membrane
Windows & Doors: Sliding Marvin
Hardware: Door Schlage
Ceilings: Exposed fir rafters and plywood sheathing
Cabinetwork: Cherry
Flooring: Oak

222

REINVENTING THE MODERN

Floors: custom carpet, stone, quarry tile
Ceiling: drywall
furniture (room by room); by owner
walls: concrete stucco
Roof: built-up membrane
Stair: aluminum
Inside structure: Structural: steel Ornamental/Detail: aluminum
artworks: by owner
windows: custom aluminum and glass
doors: solid core wood doors
Swimming pool: painted concrete
Terrace: stained cedar deck
Garage Door: sandblasted Lexan and aluminum

DOMESTIC COUNTERPOINT

The sheating (skin) of the original farm house, and the (hopefully) invisible modifications which we made to it, are clapboard. The link piece which connects the new living room addition and master bedroom addition to the farmhouse, as well as as the chimney, is horizontally oriented corrugated aluminum, a modern interpretation of clapboard. The solid walls of the living room are stucco clad, and the curved curtain wall is a Kawneer window system. The master bedroom is clad in vertically oriented, painted cedar. The roof both the living room and master bedroom are lead-coated copper. The roof on the farm house is the original slate roof. The garage roof is asphalt shingles. The large windows on the back of the house, as well as the large master bedroom windows, are by Kawneer. The smaller windows are custom wood windows from Marvin. The doors are all custom. The glass block is PPG . The pool walls are stucco. The new garage is clapboard.

The floors in the living room addition are wide plank pine. The floors in the master bedroom suite are carpet. The ceilings throughout are gypsum board except the sloped portion of the living room ceiling and the curved master bedroom ceiling, which are painted mahogany. The structure of the addition is steel, with glued-laminated beams supporting the master bedroom roof.

The stair rail on the steps into the living room is cracked glass. The bathroom walls and floor are terrazzo tile Cabinets throughout the house are custom made of painted-wood, except for the kitchen cabinets which are laminate.

The very large paintings in the living room and library are by John Walker. The suite of 6 prints in the living room are by Louise Nevelson. The small scultpure in the case near the Nevelson prints is Pre-Columbian, from Peru. The small round print in the library is by Sam Francis. The statue in the living room is a Khmer Vishnu. The mask above the Albini desk is from Zaire. One statue in the master bedroom is a Thai Buddha and the other is a Khmer piece. Outside, in front of the house, the kinetic sculpture is by Lin Emery and the low steel sculpture is by Peter Reginato. The piece between the living room and the pond is by George Rickey.

ARCHITECTURAL STAGE SETS

Owner: Architects' own house
Architect: Hideaki Ariizumi (project architect), Glynis M. Berry (associate architect)
Design Team: Guy Norderson (structural), Martin D. Gehner (structural), Sar Saratovsky (mechanical)
General Contractor: Michael Verity

Site Location: Orient, New York
Program: Single-family house with two bedrooms (one of which is subdividable) studio/office and multiple indoor/outdoor connections. An independent two-car garage/greenhouse.
Square footage: 1.450 sq.ft. (net), 1750 sq.ft.(gross).
Structural system: Wood platform framing on reinforced concrete foundation
Mechanical System: Hot water baseboard heating with supplemental fan convection heaters.
Major Exterior Materials: Asphalt shingles (roof); Clear anodized corrugated aluminum sheet by Long Island Tinsmith ("L"-walls); White cedar shingles (non "L" walls). Red cedar decking on CCA frames (deck).
Major Interior Materials: Birch plywood ("L"-walls and ceilings); Gypsum wall board (non "L"-walls and ceilings); Ash flooring (floor); White pine (window sill base, and edge trim for the "L" s); Birch, ash, and/or maple plywood (cabinetry)
Furnishings and cabinetry: Designed and built by architects.

Windows, Doors and Hardware: Standard windows and patio doors, and custom fixed frames by Pella Corporation.
Fixtures: American Standard (Kitchen, bathrooms).
Appliance & Equipment: Amana (refrigerator/freezer), GE (stove/oven), Maytag (washing machine and dryer), Broan (range hood), Arrow by Heatilator (wood stove).
Cost 212,000 USD (house including cabinetry).

BIOGRAFIE
BIOGRAPHIES

Agrest & Gandelsonas Architects
740 Broadway New York, NY 10003
tel 212-2609100 fax 212-2605661
E-mail: mgndlsns@phoenix.Princeton.EDU

Diana I. Agrest, AIA

Diana Agrest is a practicing architect in New York City. She is a principal of Agrest and Gandelsonas, Architects and she also has her own firm, Diana Agrest, Architect in New York City.

Diana Agrest has been involved in the design and building of projects in the USA, Europe and South America, ranging from single family houses and interiors to buildings, urban design projects and master plans, since 1975 and has won awards for various projects. She is the Design Director of the Des Moines Vision Plan.

She is a Professor of Architecture at Columbia University and at The Cooper Union in New York City. She has taught at Princeton University, both as full time faculty and as a Visiting Professor, and has been a Bishop Professor at Yale University. From 1972 to 1984 she was a fellow at The Institute for Architecture and Urban Studies in New York, where she was also the Director of the Advanced Design Workshop in Architecture and Urban Form.

In 1992-93 she created and directed "Framing the City: Film, Video, Urban Architecture" a post graduate course sponsored by New York University, The Rockfeller Foundation and The Whitney Museum.

Her work has been exhibited in museums and art galleries in USA, Europe and South America where she has also lectured extensively.

Both her work and writings have been widely published nationally and internationally in journals and books including Progressive Architecture, Architectural Record, Architecture and Urbanism, Architectural Design, Planning, Lotus, Oppositions, Architectural Digest, HG, Design Quarterly, etc.

She has published: The Sex of Architecture, Ed. Agrest/Conway/Weisman, Harry N. Abrams, 1996 - Agrest and Gandelsonas Works , Princeton Architectural Press, 1994 - Architecture from Without: Theoretical Framings for a Critical Practice, MIT Press, 1991 - A Romance with the City, The Work of Irwin S. Chanin, The Cooper Union, 1982

Diana Agrest received her Diploma Architect from the School of Architecture and Urbanism, University of Buenos Aires. She did post-graduate work at the Ecole Pratique des Hautes Etudes and at the Centre de Recherche d'Urbanisme in Paris 1967-1969. She is a registered architect in the State of New York, she is a member of the AIA and an American Citizen.

224

Mario Gandelsonas is a practicing architect in New York City. Since 1975 he has designed and built a wide range of projects including houses, interiors, urban buildings, master plans and urban projects. He has been a principal of Agrest and Gandelsonas Architects since 1979.

From 1971 to 1984 he was a Fellow at the Institute for Architecture and Urban Studies and the Director of Educational Programs. From 1973 to 1984 he was founder and editor of Oppositions. He is presently a member of the editorial board for Assemblage Magazine, published by MIT Press.

He was a fellow at the Institute of Architecture and Urbanism at the S.O.M. Foundation, Chicago from 1988 to 1990. He has taught at Yale, Harvard, the University of Illinois and the University of Southern California. He has lectured and given seminars at major American, European and Asian Universities. He is currently a Professor of Architecture at the Princeton University School of Architecture.

Since 1984 he has developed techniques for the formal analysis of American cities that served as a basis for a new concept of vision planning. He was the director of the Des Moines Vision Plan from 1990 to 1992 and he is currently developing a Vision Plan and Master Plan for Red Bank, New Jersey.

His articles and designs have been widely published in many national and international magazines and in several anthologies including Progressive Architecture, Architectural Record, Architectural Design, Lotus, Dolus, Design Quarterly, Space Design, A&U and Oppositions. His book, The Urban Text, SOM Foundation / MIT Press, 1991, presents a series of computer generated analytical urban drawings preceded by a collection of critical articles. The monograph Agrest and Gandelsonas, Works , Princeton Architectural Press, was recently published. The Order of the American City, Princeton Architectural Press, will be published in the Fall of 1997

Mario Gandelsonas completed his graduate studies at the School of Architecture and Urbanism, University of Buenos Aires and his post-graduate studies in Paris at the Centre de Recherche d'Urbanisme in 1967-1968. He is a Registered Architect in the State of New York.

Architrope
Andrew Bishop Bartle e Jonathan Kirschenfeld Architects
225 Lafayette Street, New York, NY 10012
tel. 212-219.8008 fax 212-219.8069

Architrope is a young, award-winning architectural firm known for its contextual approach to design problems. It was founded in 1986 by partners Andre Bartle and Jonathan Kirschenfeld, both graduates of Master of Architecture program at Princeton University. Along with the professional practice of Architecture, the partners have pursued a variety of aspects of architectural design: teaching and lecturing on architectural design and history, writing for national and international magazines, working to develop housing prototypes. The firm's design work has received recognition from the American Institute of Architects and in international competitions, and has been featured in international, national and New York design publications. Architrope was the recipient of a 1991 Distinguished Architecture Citation given by the New York City Chapter of the American Institute of Architects for the Mosley House and Studio Canaan, New York. The firm was one of the of the youngest ever to receive the award. Architrope has also won international recognition as a finalist out of over three hundred entries in the 1991 Premio Internazionale di Architettura, an extremely prestigious European architecture prize awarded in Italy. In 199 Architrope was awarded the New York City Art Commission Award for the sensitive handling of a renovation to the Brooklyn Army Terminal, a landmark building in Brooklyn, New York.

Architrope provides design services for public agencies, not-for profit institutions, corporations, educational facilities, and private clients. We have recently completed a 48-Bed SRO residence prototype for the New York State Office of Mental Health, and a Multi-purpose facility for the Berkshire Country day School in Lenox, Massachusetts. We are beginning the bidding phase for a new 15.000 sq. ft. Day Care Facility for the City of New York and have recently completed day care facility for the Economic Development Corporation in New York City. We have also produced a schematic design for a new Dormitory and outdoor Theater for Music Mountain Inc. a not-for-profit chamber music and school in Falls Village, Connecticut. Architrope recently completed projects for the Federal Express Corporation, private developers and private residential clients in New York, New Jersey, Massachusetts, and Connecticut. The majority of Architrope's work is located in New York and New England, and we have also worked on projects in Europe and California.

Eric J. Cobb
E. Cobb Architects
1306 Western Avenue #303
Seattle, Washington 98101
tel 206-287.0136 fax 206-233.9742
E-mail: ecobb@ix.netcom.com

Eric Jan Cobb received his Bachelors of Art in Architecture from the University of Washington in 1984, and his Masters in Architecture from Columbia University in 1990 with Honor for Excellence in Design. Prior to opening his own firm in 1995, he was Project Architect at Smith-Miller+Hawkinson Architects for four years, responsible for Continental Airlines Facilities Program, Newline Cinema East, Telluride Building, MaxMin House, and Corning Glass Center. In 1990, he worked for Richard Meier on the Den Haag Civic Center.

E. Cobb Architects in Seattle was established to address highly specific, challenging projects with unusual needs. Several of his projects have incorporated very difficult site and zoning conditions into remarkable project assets. His recent projects include the Creighton Residence and Kindblade Structure. Currently, the Bruckner Residence on Whidbey Island is in design, with construction scheduled for 1998.

David Coleman Architecture
1932 First Avenue, Seattle Washington 98101
tel.206-443.5626 fax 206-728.2318

David Coleman/Architecture is a nationally recognized design firm focusing on distinguished projects for residential, commercial and institutional clients. They offer a holistic approach to design, and incorporate a broad range of services including interior design, furniture design, landscape design and planning, as well as architectural design. This allows them to provide their clients with a thematic continuity of vision not often seen in this age of specialization.

Born and raised in New York, David Coleman, principal of DCA, studied fine art and environmental design at Pratt Institute before taking up architecture at the Rhode Island School of Design. He completed his studies at the Royal Danish Academy of Fine Arts, School of Architecture, focusing on community design and town & country planning.

Named in 1991 by "Architectural Digest" as one of the 100 foremost architects in the world, David brings a deep commitment to design excellence to his work. This has precipitated a broad range of professional experience throughout the United States and Europe, including extensive research in Scandinavia, a position designing for Michael Graves and a prominent commission in the highly acclaimed town of Seaside, Florida. Originally established in New England in 1986, DCA has since expanded to the Pacific Northwest. David divides his time between both coast

We approach design from a "comprehensive" point-of-view. A building or object is a component of a lerger fabric, wheteher it sists on a busy street or among the pines of the great north woods. Every design has an "opportunity" to enhance its immediate environment and to inspire its audience, regardless of its location, scale or cost. This is where the "creative process" begins.
We believe that design is much more than the application of "style" or the simple ulfillment of basic needs. Whether it involves the design of a comfortable inteior, the shape and color of a villa on the side of a hill, the texture of a facade along a city street, or the creation of a successful town plan, there is no substitue for vision, and no greater reward than the resulting richness and "beauty".

Edward I. Mills & Associates
Architects, pc
50 White Street
New York, NY 10013
Tel 212 334-9891 Fax 212 334-8197
E-mail: ElMills@aol.com

Education
Master of Architecture, with Honors
Harvard University, 1977
Bachelor of Architecture, with Honors
North Carolina State University, 1966
Architectural registrations
New York, Massachusetts, New Jersey, and Pennsylvania
Professional affiliations
American Institute of Architects
Architectural League of New York
New York Foundation for Architecture
Illuminating Engineering Society
National Council of Architectural Registration Boards
Institute of Store Planners
Marquis Who's Who in America, 1982-1983

Professional experience

1978 to Present	EDWARD I. MILLS & ASSOCIATES, ARCHITECTS, P.C. Principal
	PGE-MILLS ASSOCIATES Principal
	VOORSANGER & MILLS ASSOCIATES, ARCHITECTS, P.C. Principal
1978	RICHARD MEIER, ARCHITECT New York, New York Project Architect
1977-1978	DAVIS BRODY & ASSOCIATES New York, New York Project Architect, Project Designer
1971-1976	I.M.PEI & PARTNERS, ARCHITECTS New York, NY Project Architect, Project Designer
1969-1970	RICHARD KAPLAN, ARCHITECT New York, NY Project Designer:
1966-1968	U.S. ARMY CORPS OF ENGINEERS 1st Lieutenant
1966	THE ARCHITECTS COLLABORATIVE Cambridge, Massachusettes Project Architect, Project Designer

Supplemental information
Vice-President, NYC Chapter, American Institute of Architects, NYC Chapter 1995-1997
Member, Board of Directors, American Institute of Architects NYC Chapter,
1995-1997
Member, Board of Directors, Illuminating Engineering Society, NYC Chapter
1988-1996
Member, Board of Trustees, New York Foundation for Architecture, 1996
Member, Long Island, NY Chapter AIA Awards Jury, 1992
Chairman, Program Committee, Illuminating Engineering Society,1992
Chairman, AIA National Action for Better Government, 1990
Chairman, Lumen Awards Committee, Illuminating Engineering Society,1988,1990
Chair, Dialogue Committee, AIA NYC Chapter, 1988-1990
Member, Planning Committee, Architectural Art Exhibit, American Crafts Museum, New York, New York, 1987-1988

Chairman, AIA NYC Chapter Awards Committee, 1987-1988
Member, Brunner AIA NYC Chapter Awards Committee, 1987
Member, Jacksonville, Florida Award Jury, 1986
Co-Chairman, AIA NYC Chapter Awards Committee, 1986
Member, AIA NYC Chapter Awards Committee, 1985-1986
Member, AIA Texas State Awards Jury, 1985
Member, AIA NYC Chapter Interiors Committee, 1983-1985
Member, Steering Committee, Institute of Architecture and Urban Studies, 1984-1985
Member, AIA Denver Chapter Award Jury, 1983
Member, Express Network Advisory Committee, 1982
Member, AIA NYC Chapter Stewardson Traveling Fellowship Committee, 1979-80
Member, AIA NYC Chapter Housing Committee, 1979-1983
Member, Advisory Board, SoHo Community Council, 1996-1997
Visiting professor
University of Miami at Oxford, Ohio, 1987
Syracuse University, Spring 1986
Columbia University, Spring 1985
Yale University, Spring 1984
Columbia University, Spring 1983
Rhode Island School of Design, Fall 1981
University of Pennsylvania, Fall 1979
Guest critic and lecturer
Architecture League of New York, The
Carnegie-Mellon University
City College, NY,NY
Columbia University
Cooper Union
Cornell University
Fashion Institute of Technology
Harvard University
Institute of Architecture and Urban Studies, The (NY, NY)
Institute of Store Planners, The (NY, NY)
Lawrence Institute of Architecture, Detroit, Michigan
New Jersey Institute of Technology
New York Institute of Technology
North Carolina State University
Parsons School of Design
Pratt Institute
Rhode Island School of Design
Syracuse University
University of Colorado, Boulder
University of Miami at Ohio
University of Pennsylvania
University of Toronto, Canada
Yale University
Panel discussions
"Architectural Lighting," Parsons School of Design, 1993
"Meet the Stars," Designers of Lighting Fixtures New York, 1992
"Architectural Education," AIA Chapter, 1991
"Art as Architecture," AIA NYC Chapter, 1990
"Lighting," Illuminating Engineering Society, 1989
"Licensing for Interior Designers," The International Design Center, 1987
"The Business of Design," Colorado State AIA, 1986
"Lighting Design Round Table," Architectural Record, 1985
"Architectural Facades," Institute of Architecture and Urban Studies, NY, NY, 1985
"The Architecture of Display Showrooms," The Architectural League, 1982
"The Small Interior Firm," AIA NYC Chapter, 1981
Exhibits designed
"New York Architecture," Whitney Museum, 1989
"Architectural Art," American Craft Museum, 1988
"New York Architecture," Max Protech Gallery, 1988
Exhibitions
"Civics Lessons," Civic Architecture NY, NY,1996
"Tower 2000," Salvadori Educational Center, 1994
"Art in Architecture," Port Washington, NY, 1994
"City-Room-Garden," Travelling Exhibition, 1993
"New York Police Academy Competition," Architectural League, 1993
"New York Police Academy Competition," Pratt Institute, Brooklyn, 1993
"New York Police Academy Competition," Police Headquarters Bldg.,1993
"Architects for S.O.S.," Drawing Exhibition, NY, 1992
"Art in Architecture," Port Washington, NY, 1991
"Mailbox Auction," Smithsonian Institution, 1992
"CAYC," Buenos Aires Biennale 1991, Buenos Aires, Brazil
"MASK," Dynasen Gallery New York, NY, 1991
"East Hampton Airport Competition," New York Institute of Technology School of Architecture, 1990
"New York Architecture," National Academy of Design, 1990
"East Hampton Airport Competition," The National Institute for Architectural

Education, 1990
"New York Architects," Whitney Museum, 1989
"Beaux-Arts V," Bridgehampton, New York, 1989
"Reweaving the Urban Fabric: International Approaches to Infill Housing," New York Council of the Arts
"Faculty Work," Syracuse University, 1987
"Bird Houses by Architects," Parrish Art Museum, Southhampton, New York, 1987
"Vacant Lots," Architectural League, New York, 1987
"Edward Mills: Drawing," AIA NYC Chapter, New York, 1986
"Beaux-Arts III," Bridgehampton, New York, 1985
"Architects for Social Responsibility Auction Show," New York, 1984-87
"University of Florida Art Museum Competition," Gainesville, Florida, 1985
"Faculty Work," Columbia University, New York, 1985
"The Work of Voorsanger & Mills," Architectural Association,London, England, 1984
"Faculty Work," Yale University, 1985
"The Work of Edward Mills," Fox Gallery, Denver, Colorado, 1984
"Carnegie Mansion: Embellishments," Cooper-Hewitt Museum, New York, 1983
"Creation and Recreation: America Draws," Louisiana Museum,Denmark, 1982
"Modern Citizens Against Post Modernism," Express/Network, New York, 1982
"The Work of Voorsanger & Mills," N.Y.U. School of Business,New York 1981
"Artists and Architects: Collaboration," The Architectural League, New York Historical Society, New York, 1981
"Window, Room Furniture," Cooper Union New York, 1981
"Creation and Recreation: America Draws," Museum of Finnish Architecture, Helsinki, 1980

Marlys Hann Architect
52 West 84th Street New York, NY 10024
tel. 212-787.1680
fax 212- 787.1719

Marlys Hann is a licensed architect who has the additional special talent for creating exceptional interior spaces. She has a wonderfully creative conceptual ability joined with a persistent and refined attention to detail and the perseverance to see a project through from beginning to end so that it provides the most satisfaction for client, designer and builder alike.

226   Since 1976 she has led her own firm whose main purpose is to produce a high level of design quality .... Architecture with poetry and elegance combined with careful attention to real needs and requirements, budgets, and intended completion dates.

She originally graduated Phi Beta Kappa with B.A. from the University of Oregon and an M.F.A. from Pratt Institute. She has served as a design instructor at Pratt Institute and Parsons School of Design, and as the coordinator of the Interior Deisgn Program in the School of Architecture at the University of Southwestern Louisiana. She was a panelist on the New York State Council of the Arts (NYSCA) Architecture and Design Review Board.

Previous to starting her own practice, she was an associate at Ford and Earl Design Associates, where she was responsible for the design of special corporate projects including the RCA Conference Center, a unique project combining rooftop construction, glass-enclosed garden and walkways, top management board room and dining rooms with high technology audio-visual facilities.

Her past projects have also yielded special experience in store design and in custom residences, renovation, restoration and interiors. Marlys Hann, one of five architects to receive the "Excellence in Design" award from the New York Association of Architects, AIA, for her "Stone House" and one of her designs was also selected for "Best Small House" in a competition sponsored by *House Beautiful* and the American Wood Council.

Marlys Hann designs facilities which are efficient to operate and fit pleasingly into their contexts. She is knowledgeable in the use of non-toxic and ecologically friendly building materials and methods. She believes environmentally conscious and responsible construction can best be achieved by working in close partnership with the client, specialized consultants, and builders in all phases of a project in order to find solutions that are innovative, buildable and beautiful.

Michael Graves Architect
341 Nassau Street, Princeton, New Jersey 08540
Tel. 609-924.6409 fax 609-924.1795
E-mail: MGAPrince@aol.com

Michael Graves has been in the forefront of architectural design since he began his practice in Princeton, New Jersey in 1964. Paul Goldberger, architectural critic of *The New York Times*, has said that "Graves .... is truly the most original voice America has produced in some time." He has received over 100 prestigious awards for his designs in architecture, interiors, products, and graphics, and

has come to enjoy an international reputation.

Among his completed projects in the United States alone are: corporate headquarters for Humana, Crown American, the Disney Company, and Thomson Consumer Electronics. Other built projects include: the Portland Building; the Clos Pegase Winery in the Napa Valley; the Walt Disney World Dolphin and Swan Hotels in Orlando; and the Aventine hotel and office building complex in La Jolla, California. Public cultural institutions include the Denver Central Library; the Clark County Library and Theater in Las Vegas; the San Juan Capistrano Library; and the Riverbend Music Center in Cincinnati.

Graves' practice has become highly international, with the completion, for example, in Japan of major projects such as the Tajima Building; headquarters for Kasumi; a town hall at Onjuku; residential towers in Yokohama and Fukuoka and the Fukuoka Hyatt Regency Hotel and office building, among many. In Europe, projects include the Hotel New York at Disneyland Park Paris; a hotel and office building in Antwerp, Belgium; and an office building for the Ministry of Culture in The Hague.

Graves is also well known for his design of furniture, furnishings, and artifacts including furniture for various manufacturers, table top items and decorative accessories for Alessi, carpets for Vorwerk; and floor tiles for Tajima.

Graves' work appears in many periodicals and books, including *Five Architects* published in 1972 by Oxford University Press; *Michael Graves*, published in 1979 by Academy Editions; *Michael Graves: Building and Projects 1966-1981* published in 1983 by Rizzoli; *Michael Graves: Buildings and Projects 1982-1989*, published in 1990 by The Princeton Architectural Press; and *Michael Graves Design Monograph*, published in 1994 by Ernst & Sohn. A new monograph covering architectural projects from 1990-1994 was published by Rizzoli in 1995.

Michael Graves received his architectural training at the University of Cincinnati and Harvard University. In 1960, he won the Rome Prize and studied at The American Academy in Rome, of which he is now a Trustee. Graves is the Schirmer Professor of Architecture at Princeton University, where he has taught since 1962.

Pasanella, Klein, Stolzman, Berg Architects
330 West 42nd. St., New York NY 10036
tel. 212-5942010 fax 212-947.4381
E-mail: 74672.3300@CompuServe.COM

Wayne Berg, FAIA

Wayne Berg's extensive bibliography of published work, his election to 40 under 40 and Emerging Voices, and his American Institute of Architects Design Awards testify to the level of recognition he has received for his design achievements.

His work is characterized by intense attention to detail, material, and craft. This attention is applied to projects that range in scale and function from the 6 1/2' high birdhouse built for the Parish Art Museum to the Education and Development Center at Clinch Valley College, University of Virginia.

Wayne Berg's buildings and interiors respond to and enrich the context they inhabit. Some mediate between conflicting architectural voices that surround them; some speak assertively as the principal character; others engage in a more quiet dialogue. In all cases, Berg's sensitive, judicious, and respectful handling of each new structure as a part of an evolving whole has created buildings and interiors that belong to their historical and physical environments.

Wayne Berg is currently at work on PS/IS 89, a new 102,000 square foot public school in Battery Park City, Lower Manhattan; the conversion of Columbia's McKim Mead & White Journalism building to a multimedia teaching, production and broadcast facility; Stabile Hall, a new dormitory for Pratt Institute; and a house in Westchester County, New York. Recently, he has completed the 42,000 square foot Addition to Reed Library at the State University of New York College at Fredonia, the new Chemical Engineering and Biotechnology Building (Phase I) at UVA Charlottesville and the Physics Building Addition on the same campus.

Wayne has served his colleagues and the profession through the AIA's New York Chapter. He has been its Vice President, Chair of the Design Awards Committee and Editor of New York Architecture Volume 4, a member of Oculus, and a member of the Nominating Committee. He worked on the educational architecture task force formed by the NYC School Construction Authority and the AIA/NYC. He was named a Fellow in the Institute this year. Wayne is also a participant in the Regional Plan Association, which recently completed the Manhattan Crosstown Regional Plan.

A native of Montana, Wayne received his Bachelor of Architecture from Montana State University in 1969. Wayne Berg has been Adjunct Assistant Professor at Columbia University's Graduate School of Architecture, Planning and Preservation for the past five years.

Albert Ho, AIA

Albert Ho joined PKSB in 1990 and was named an Associate in 1993. Before joining the firm, he worked at Schwartz/Silver Architects in Boston, serving as Project Architect for the Wheeler School Library Addition in Providence, Rhode sland. As a recent architecture graduate, Albert worked with many top architects in the US and Asia, including Fred Koetter and Raphael Moneo. Albert received his Master of Architecture degree from Harvard University Graduate School of Design in 1986 and won Second Prize in the 1989 Literary House Competition. Today, Albert Ho teaches and practices in Taipei, Taiwan.

Peter Forbes and Associates Inc.
70 Long Wharf, Boston Massachusetts 02110
tel. 617-523.5800 fax 617-523.5810
E-mail: PFABOS@TIAC.NET

Peter Forbes and Associates, Inc. was founded in 1980 by Peter Forbes, FAIA , with offices in Boston, Massachusetts. Within four years the firm had expanded its practice, opened branch offices in Maine and New York City and was engaged in projects throughout the United States. Since that time Peter Forbes and Associates have become celebrated for their architecture of rigorously simple forms carefully sited in the landscape and meticulously detailed.

The firm was first recognized by the cover story in *Architectural Record* magazine of December 1981, followed by Record House Awards in 1983, 1986, 1987 and 1989. In 1986 Peter Forbes and Associates received the National Honor Award for a house designed on Deer Isle, Maine, only the third National Honor Award ever given to a building in Maine and still the only such award given to a house in Maine. With the extensive publication of this house throughout the world architectural press and its subsequent receipt of six additional awards, Peter Forbes and Associates became established as one of a very few firms who primarily focus on residential architecture at the highest level of design. They were further distinguished in an era of fleetingly transient fashions in design as a firm committed to timeless architecture, neither trendy nor historicist, excellently constructed of materials that would endure. For this work the firm has received over thirty design awards and has been extensively published in periodicals and professional journals in America, Europe and Asia.

Throughout the history of the firm, Peter Forbes and Associates have been selected to design a variety of building types, commercial, institutional and public as well as residential. The common denominator of these commissions and the resulting buildings has been an imperative to evolve innovative solutions to design problems that have few, if any, precedents. Whether the program demanded an exploration of alternative materials to produce a toxin-free environment or the invention of low energy, low environmental impact structures for the military, or an urban residential prototype that mitigated the effects of dense urban settlement and noise—including the now ubiquitous intrusion of aircraft sound— these were not conditions that could be resolved through the reiteration of formal preconceptions. Each of these, and similar demands, required an independence from reliance upon past solutions. Each necessitated intense analysis of program, client and site specifics, often resulting in the development of innovative materials, systems and fabrication techniques. Peter Forbes and Associates approach architecture without stylistic "baggage", achieving new solutions to complex problems from within the needs and desires of the client and the dictates of the site.

As important as their involvement is with technical innovation, Peter Forbes and Associates is equally engaged in re-examining the cultural parameters that underlie society's need for architecture. The basic tenet of their architecture is that to design is, in essence, to explain: the function, the role or the meaning of the designed object in its universe. Only through its relationship to the orders, ceremonies and beliefs of a culture can technical innovation achieve meaning beyond the most immediate functional response. Only when design is in resonance with intrinsic human concerns, not superficial preconceptions, can it ascend from mere shelter to genuine architecture. This resonance is constantly changing; its determination, a constant search. That exploration is what the architecture of Peter Forbes and Associates is about.

Peter L. Gluck Architect
Peter Gluck & Partners
19 Union Square West, New York, NY 10003
tel. 212-2551876 fax 212-6330144
E-mail pgluck@inch.com

Peter Gluck received a B.A. from Yale University and a Master of Architecture from the Yale School of Art and Architecture in 1965. After designing a series of houses from New York to Newfoundland, he went to Tokyo to design large projects for a leading Japanese construction consortium. This experience influenced Gluck's later work both in his knowledge of Japan's traditional aesthetics and of its efficient modern methods of integrated construction and design.

Located in New York City since 1972, the practice of Peter L. Gluck and Partners is known for its integrity of design and sensitivity to the relationship between architectural form and architectural context. The firm has designed buildings throughout the United States, ranging in type from hotels, schools, university buildings, and churches to houses, corporate interiors, and historic restorations. Gluck's belief that the architect must take responsibility for the architectural process from conception to construction has led to his assuming oversight of all aspects of design. The same commitment led him to establish ARCS (Architectural Construction Services), Inc., an integrated system of architectural design and construction management, which provides his clients with sophisticated design, quality construction, and cost management in an increasingly difficult building environment.

Exhibitions of Gluck's award-winning work have been held in the U.S. and Japan. He is widely published around the world and has taught at Columbia and Yale schools of architecture. He has also curated museum exhibitions, including Shinjuku: The Phenomenal City, on Japanese urbanism at the Museum of Modern Art in 1976, and Globalization and Regionalism, which commemorated American schools of architecture at the Milan Triennale of 1996.

Peter Samton Architect
304 Park Avenue South, New York, New York
10010-5302
tel. 212-4770900 fax 212-477.1257
E-mail 102024.2434@compuserve.com

Peter Samton, FAIA
Partner
Gruzen Samton

Personal
Born: February 26, 1935, Berlin, Germany
immigrated 1939; Naturalized U.S. Citizen, 1944
Married to Emily Leshan Samton, 1963
Children: Zach, Noah and Daniel

Education
Stuyvesant High School, 1952
Massachusetts Institute of Technology, Bachelor of Architecture, 1957
- Grunsfeld Traveling Fellowship (M.I.T.), 1956
- Tau Beta Pi, Honor Engineering Society
- AIA Silver Medal for Scholarship
Fulbright Fellowship in Architecture, Paris, France, 1957-1958
CIAM School in Venice, Fall 1958

Registrations
Registered Architect in New York, New Jersey, Massachusetts and Virginia - NCARB

Career profile
After completing a year as a Fulbright Fellow in France, Mr. Samton worked for the Danish firm of Gunnlogsson and Nielsen on the Toronto City Hall Competition - they were selected as one of six finalists. Returning to the U.S. in 1959 for a brief service in the U.S. Army, Mr. Samton worked for Hugh Stubbins 1959-1960, and then for Marcel Breuer 1960-1962. In 1961 he, together with A.W. Geller and Claude Samton, entered the FDR Memorial Competition and became one of six finalists. In 1962 Mr. Samton became a registered Architect, and in 1963, after a brief stint in private practice, he joined the firm of Kelly & Gruzen. The firm became Gruzen and Partners in 1967, and Mr. Samton became a Partner.

In 1970 Mr. Samton became Design Director of the firm, overseeing the entire design process. He was in charge of the design of New York City Police Headquarters. A planning and urban design studio was added in 1975, and the firm became involved in large-scale planning projects in the New York area and abroad. In 1980, the Gruzen Partnership opened an office in San Francisco and a new office in New Jersey. In 1986 the firm split, with the largest portion becoming Gruzen Samton Steinglass Architects, Planners & Interior Designers practice, which has now evolved into Gruzen Samton. A new office was added in Washington DC, increasing the overall staff to 80 people. The firm is responsible for many of New York City's major buildings, including schools, hotels, apartment houses, court facilities etc. Mr. Samton is currently collaborating with Bernard Tschumi on a major new Student Center for Columbia University. In 1993 Mr. Samton became the Managing Partner and Chief Executive Officer.

Professional and civic activities
Fellow: American Institute of Architects (FAIA)
President: New York Chapter of the AIA, 1977-1978
President: City Club of New York 1989-1991
Chairperson of the Planning and Zoning Committee, City Club of New York, 1983-89

Honors and awards
4 National AIA Honor Awards - 1964, 1968, 1981, 1991
6 New York State AIA Awards including 1995 Honor Award for PS 51
7 City Club of New York Bard Awards for Excellence in Architecture,1967, 1973, 1975, 1977, 1979, 1981, 1988
NYC Chapter AIA Medal of Honor, 1974 (Gruzen & Partners)
NYC Chapter AIA Pioneer in Housing Award, 1985
NYC Chapter AIA President's Award for Contributions to the City and the

Profession, 1988
NYC Chapter AIA Harry B. Rutkins Award for Service to the Profession, 1992
NYC Chapter AIA Design Award Citation for Stuyvesant High School, NY, 1994
3 Bronze Plaques - Municipal Art Society for Architectural Excellence, 1969, 1971, 1973
B'nai B'rith International Distinguished Achievement Award, 1989
State of Israel Bonds Gates of Jerusalem Medal 1995
Numerous other civic, community and professional awards.

Schwarzt/Silver Architects Inc
530 Atlantic Ave, Boston Massachusetts 02210
tel. 717-542.6650 fax 617-951.0779
E-mail ARCH@SCHWARTZSILVER.COM

Schwartz/Silver has earned international recognition as a new voice in American architecture and interior design.
The firm's work has been featured in books and magazines in the U.S., Italy, France, Germany, England, and Japan.
Recent awards include four national awards from the American Institute of Architects, six Honor Awards from the Boston Society of Architects, two Gold Medals from the Boston Society of Architects for the most beautiful buildings in the Boston area, six regional architecture awards, and four national awards for interior design.
The buildings Schwartz/Silver designs are widely recognized for their innovation and vitality. Projects of note include:

The New England Aquarium Boston, Massachusetts USA

The Crayola Factory Children's Museum Easton, Pennsylvania USA

The Delta Aviation Museum ,Atlanta, Georgia USA

Massachusetts Institute of Technology Library of Art, Architecture and Planning Cambridge, Massachusetts USA

Smith-Miller + Hawkinson Architects
305 Canal Street New York, New York 10013
tel.212-966.3875 fax 212-966.3877
E-mail: TAYLOR@smharch.com

Smith-Miller + Hawkinson Architects, founded in 1977, is an architectural firm with offices in New York and Los Angeles (since 1989). The firm consists of two principals, Henry Smith-Miller and Laurie Hawkinson, and twenty-two employees in New York and two employees in Los Angeles.
Smith-Miller + Hawkinson's projects span a very wide scope, from small to very large and complex interiors, from additions to free-standing single or multi-use structures.
Smith-Miller + Hawkinson bring to the firm strong interests in a general culture of architecture: its design and technological histories, as well as its complex and changing relationship to society. Of these changes, the firm is particularly interested in focusing on the ways in which the architectural program – the location and accommodation of functions, activities, and services – can be developed through innovative interpretations that are sensitive to and transformative of contemporary cultural needs and ideas.

Henry Smith-Miller, Partner in Charge. An Architect and principal in the office of Smith-Miller + Hawkinson; he began his private practice in 1977 following a seven year association with Richard Meier and Associates where he was a project architect for several nationally recognized architectural projects: The Athaneum at New Harmony Indiana, the Albany Mall Art Museum, and the Bronx Developmental Center. He received an undergraduate degree from Princeton University, a Masters in Architecture from the Graduate School of Architecture at the University of Pennsylvania, and a Fulbright Grant to study architecture in Rome, Italy. Henry Smith-Miller has held visiting adjunct professor positions at Columbia University, the City University of New York, the University of Virginia, the University of Pennsylvania, Harvard University, the Thomas Jefferson Professor in Architecture at the University of Virginia, and the Saarinen Chair at Yale University. He has recently taught a graduate studio with Kenneth Frampton at Columbia University. He has also served on the Board of Creative Time and is a member of the Associate Council of the Museum of Modern Art in New York. Collaborative projects include the exhibition design for Discontinuous Space: Projects by Smith-Miller + Hawkinson Architects with artist Silvia Kolbowski. He is a registered Architect in New York, Pennsylvania, Maryland, Connecticut, California, North Carolina, Virginia, Maine, Colorado, NCARB Certification.

Laurie Hawkinson An Architect and principal in the office of Smith-Miller + Hawkinson; she received her Masters in Fine Arts from the University of

228

California at Berkeley, then attended the Whitney Independent Study Program in New York and received her Professional Degree in Architecture from The Cooper Union in 1983. Currently an Associate Professor of Architecture at Columbia University, Laurie Hawkinson has held visiting adjunct professor positions at SCI-Arc, Harvard University, Yale University, Parsons School of Design, and the University of Miami. She is a board member of the Architectural League of New York, a member of the Board of Governors of the New York Foundation for the Arts, and has served as a panelist for the New York State Council on the Arts in Architecture, Planning and Design from 1986-1989. Collaborative projects include the North Carolina Museum of Art "Master" Site Plan and project, now built, for an outdoor cinema and amphitheater with artist Barbara Kruger and landscape architect Nicholas Quennell, LA Arts Park Competition and the Seattle Waterfront Project, also with Kruger and Quennell. She has worked with the artist Silvia Kolbowski on a project for the Wexner Center's recent exhibition on suburbia, House Rules. She is a registered Architect in New York and NCARB certified.

Stamberg & Aferiat Architects,
126 Fifth Avenue, NY,NY 10011.
tel : 212- 255 4173 - fax: 212-431 4496

Paul Aferiat
Education: Carnegie Mellon University (Architecture), Bachelor of Architecture 1975

Experience: Richard Meier & Partners, 1975-1979. Gwathmey Siegel & Associates, 1979-1989

Partial Job List: Guggenheim Museum, New York. Aye Simon Reading Room and Expansion Study. New York School of Painting, State Museum at Albany. The Athaneum, New Armony Indiana. Hartford Seminary, Hartford Connecticut. Taubman House, Palm Beach, Florida. Suarez Apt., New York. D'Arcy Masius Benton & Bowles Advertising, New York. McCann Erickson Wordliwe Advertising, New York. American Museum of the Moving Image, New York. Knoll Showroom, Chicago. Herman Miller Showroom, New York. Stending Showroom, New York. Westover School, Westover Connecticut. Greenwich Savings Bank, New York. Reliance Holdings, New York. deMenil Residence, New York. Viereck Residence, East Hampton, New York. deMenil Residence, East Hampton , New York. Opel Residence, Shelburne Vermont.

Peter Stamberg
Education: Columbia College (History of Art & Architecture), Rhode Island School of Design (Architecture). Bachelor of Fine Arts, 1972. Bachelor of Architecture, 1973. Architectural Association of London Graduate School of Architecture (Architecture & Semiotics). A.A.G. Dipl., 1974.
Experience: Atelier International (Marcatre/Cassina), New York. Wright Line Worcester, Massachusetts. Data Mate, New Hampshire. House & Garden Magazine, New York. Interiors Magazine, New York. Davis, Brody & Associates, New York.

Steven Holl Architects
435 Hudson Street New York, NY 10014
tel 212-9090918 fax 212-4639718
E-mail sha@walrus.com

Steven Holl, principal
Steven Holl (b. Bremerton, Washington, 1947) established Steven Holl Architects in New York in 1976. Holl is an honors graduate of the University of Washington. He studied architecture in Rome, Italy in 1970, and did post-graduate work at the Architectural Association in London in 1976.
In 1989, the Museum of Modern Art presented Holl's work in a special two-man show, purchasing several drawings for their permanent collection. In 1991 Holl's work was featured in a solo exhibition at the Walker Art Center in Minneapolis, in the series entitled "Architecture Tomorrow" curated by Mildred Friedman. This exhibition was moved to the Henry Art Gallery in Seattle, Washington and in 1992-3 exhibited throughout Europe. In 1992 Holl received the National AIA Interiors Award for the offices of D.E. Shaw & Co. in New York City and in 1993 the National AIA Honor Award for Excellence in Design for "Texas Stretto House" in Dallas, Texas. That same year, Steven Holl Architects was awarded the winning design among 516 entries in the competition for the new Museum of Contemporary Art, Helsinki. The project is scheduled to complete construction in January 1998. Among his most recent honors are the 1995 New York Honor Awards for Excellence in Design for "Chapel of St Ignatius" in Seattle, Washington, and the "Cranbrook Institute of Science" addition and renovation in Bloomfield Hills, Michigan. Holl's 190 unit Makuhari Housing in Chiba, Japan, which won an A.I.A. award for Design Excellence, recently completed construction in March 1996.

rofessional affiliations
CARB Registered - New York, New Jersey, California, Michigan, Washington, Ohio, Florida, Texas
American Institute of Architects
American Association of Museums
Honorary Whitney Circle, Whitney Museum of American Art

Teaching
Columbia University Graduate School of Architecture and Planning, New York
Tenured Professor since 1989; Adjunct professor since 1981
University of Washington, Seattle
Pratt Institute, New York
University of Pennsylvania, Philadelphia

Honors
1990 Arnold W. Brunner Prize for Achievement in Architecture as an Art - American Academy and Institute of Arts and Letters
TOMOAKI TANAKA, registered architect, Japan
years with Steven Holl Architects
Waseda University, Japan
Yale University School of Architecture, Honors Graduate
Project Architect: Makuhari Housing, Japan Project Team: Museum of Contemporary Art, Helsinki,
Finland; Villa den Haag, The Netherlands;

Justin Russli, registered architect, switzerland
years with Steven Holl Architects
Eidgenossische Technische Hochschule Zurich, Switzerland dipl. arch. ETH
Columbia University Graduate School of Architecture, MSAAD
Recipient of Eternit Award for Postgraduate Studies; Award for Excellence in Design, Columbia University
Project Architect: Zollikerberg Housing, Zurich; Düsseldorf Harborfront, Düsseldorf. Project Team: Museum of Contemporary Art, Helsinki

Chris Mcvoy
years with Steven Holl Architects
University of Virginia, BS Architecture
Columbia University Graduate School of Architecture
Guggenheim Studentship, 1985; William Kinne Travel Fellowship; American Scandinavian Foundation Grant
Project Architect: Cranbrook Institute of Science

Pablo Castro-Estèvez, registered architect, New York
year with Steven Holl Architects
years with Richard Meier & Partners
Universidad de San Juan, Argentina, Honors Graduate
Columbia University Graduate School of Architecture
1st Prize San José Veteran's Memorial Competition
Project Team: Museum of Contemporary Art, Helsinki, Cranbrook Institute of Science, Michigan

Janet Cross
years with Steven Holl Architects
University of California, Berkeley, BArchitecture, Suma Cum Laude
Project Designer: Walker Musuem Exhibition, Minneapolis; Z-House, Millbrook; Competition Museum of Contemporary Art, Helsinki; Third and Fourth Floor Exhibition, Whitney Museum of American Art, New York

Timothy Bade
years with Steven Holl Architects
Arizona State University, BS Architecture
Columbia University Graduate School of Architecture
Arizona AIA Travel Fellowship, McKim Prize, William Kinne Travel Fellowship
Project Architect: St. Ignatius Chapel, Seattle University, WA

Studio a/b
11 Fourth Avenue 2M
New York, NY 10003
tel & fax 212-677.7898

Established in '92 by Glynis M. Berry and Hideaki Ariizumi, practicing planning, architectural and furniture design.

Glynis Margaret Berry
Born in Providence , Rhode Island USA. Glynis Margaret Berry practices architecture in New York City Department of Transportation.
A graduate of the Smith College, with a double major in English and studio art, she worked at museums as an exhibit designer and served as a director of a children's museum before receiving her Master of Architecture degree at Yale University, School of Architecture. A recipient of a Monbusho Scholarship, she studied and practiced architecture at Tokyo Institute of Technology with Kazuo Shinohara and Kazunari Sakamoto.
Working as an urban designer with the New York City Department of Transportation, she initiated a Pedestrian Projects Group, applied for funding and established an experimental planning program. As a pioneer of pedestrian projects, she has lectured at symposiums nationwide and served on numerous advisory committees.
Architectural and furniture projects done in collaboration with her partner have been published and exhibited in the USA, Japan and abroad.

Hideaki Ariizumi
Born in Tokyo, Japan, Hideaki Ariizumi practices architecture in New York City with his firm "studio a/b", after having been an associate with Steven Holl Architects, New York, and with Kazuo Shinohara Atelier, Japan. As project architect, he guided the Fukuoka Housing Project, which was awarded both a "Progressive Architecture Citation '91" and "AIA New York Chaptor Award '92".
A graduate of the Tokyo Institute of Technology, Japan, he continued his study and practice of architecture at the university as an instructor and member of the Kazuo Shinohara Studio. He also Taught at several school in Japan as well as the New Jersey Institute of Technology.
The House on North Folk, executed by studio a/b, was awarded in Space Design (SD) Review '94. His architectural and furniture designs have been published and exhibited in the USA. Japan and abroad.

William Leddy Architect, AIA
444 Spear st., San Francisco California
tel 415 394.5400 fax 415 394.8400

William Leddy has practiced architecture in San Francisco since 1975 and has served as Vice President of Tanner Leddy Maytum Stacy Architects since 1989. His diverse body of work includes institutional, commercial, multi-family housing and single-family housing projects in both new construction and the adaptive reuse of existing and historic structures.
Mr. Leddy has been a visiting lecturer and invited critic at the Southern California Institute of Architecture, the California College of Arts & Crafts, the University of Oregon and the University of California, Berkeley. His work has received numerous local, state and national design awards and has been published extensively in the US, Japan and Europe, in magazines such as *Architectural Record, Elle Décor, Sunset, Abitare* and *Hauser*.
Mr. Leddy's work has been exhibited nationally and representative pieces are included in the permanent collection if the San Francisco Museum of Modern Art. Tanner Leddy Maytum Stacy Architects was recently profiled in "Dictionnaire de l'Architecture du XXe Siècle" an international compendium of leading architects compiled by the French Institute of Architecture.
The firm's recent local projects include the Charles B. Thornton Center for Engineering Management at Stanford University; the 112 unit Graduate Student Housing at Governor's Corner, also at Stanford University; the California College of Art & Crafts, San Francisco Campus; the Thoreau Center for Sustainability at the Presidio; offices for C/net the Computer Network and offices for Goodby Silverstein & Partners, both in San Francisco.

Fotolito: Lorenteggio - Milano
Stampa: Grafiche Alma - Milano
Legatura: Pedrelli - Parma